TOP 10 TOPICS
for School Counselors

Roxanne Zusmer

cover design by Linda Jean Thille

Copyright © 2005, INNERCHOICE PUBLISHING • All rights reserved
(Revised Edition, 2011)

ISBN – 10: 1-56499-076-1

ISBN – 13: 978-1-56499-076-1

INNERCHOICE Publishing
15079 Oak Chase Court
Wellington, FL 33414

www.InnerchoicePublishing.com

Experience sheets may be reproduced only in quantities sufficient for distribution to students in those classrooms utilizing *Top 10 Topics for School Counselors*. All other reproduction for any purpose whatsoever is explicitly prohibited without written permission. Requests for permission should be directed to INNERCHOICE PUBLISHING.

DEDICATION

To my children
Todd, Dean, and Lisa
Who have taught me so much
About life

ACKNOWLEDGMENTS

This book could not have been written without the expertise, dedication, and support of others. My gratitude is extended to:

Susanna Palomares, of Innerchoice Publishing, Inc., who understood the need for a timely, updated book; and whose belief in my efforts to write this book was unwavering. I sincerely appreciate her continuous guidance, know-how, and persistence throughout the writing process, as well as the friendship we have developed;

Linda Jean Thille, whose cover design portrayed the essence of what this book is all about, and whose graphic art enhances the pages.

All of the children who have shared with me their courage, determination, fortitude, and resilience in overcoming obstacles and barriers in their lives. It is because of them that counseling is filled with meaning;

My friends, whose enthusiasm and faith have been never ending. They all have special places in my life;

My devoted family, whose confidence and support have been, and continue to be, immeasurable; especially, to my husband, Noel, who has lovingly encouraged me onward toward accomplishing my goal.

TABLE OF CONTENTS

Introduction 1

How To Use This Book 4

1. **Self-Awareness** 7
   Pride Bingo 8
   Self-Portrait 12
   Attitude: A State of Mind 15

2. **Peer Relationships/Friendship** 19
   Compliment Bag 20
   Is Your Behavior Really You 23
   Nobody Likes Me: *Maybe They Just Don't Know You* 28

3. **Communication** 33
   Group Story 34
   Listening Skills 36
   What Is That Label You Are Wearing 38

4. **Anger/Conflict** 43
   When One Door Opens, Another One Closes 44
   Angry Words 50
   Out-Stressing Anger 54

5. **Bullying/Harassment** 57
   Communicating Feelings 58
   Bullying Behaviors 61
   Cyber-Bullying: A Powerful Bullying Tool 63

6. **Diversity/Tolerance** 65
   Stand Up and Be Counted 66
   Understanding Tolerance 69
   Getting Acquainted With Diversity 75

7.	**Goals/Organization**	83
	Using Time Wisely	84
	Thinking S.M.A.R.T.	86
	Earnest Effort	89
8.	**Transition/Mobility**	95
	Working With Immigrant Families – *Information for Counselors*	96
	Cooperative Group Picture	98
	Transition to Junior/Middle or High School	100
	Circle of Friends – *Outside/Inside*	106
9.	**Children of Divorce**	109
	It's Not Your Fault	110
	Puzzling Emotions	114
	What I Think – What I Feel	117
	Parent Permission Letter	120
10.	**Grief and Loss**	121
	Expressing Feelings of Grief and Loss	122
	Coping Skills	127
	A Chance to Say Good-bye	131
	Parent Permission Letter	135

INTRODUCTION

Life today is filled with increasing challenges and change. More than ever before, children and adolescents are dealing with insecurities, stresses, and depression in an unpredictable environment.

This book has been written to provide school counselors with an updated and timely curriculum of information and group activities to use with children and adolescents. It is our task, as educators and counseling professionals, to address the physical, social, and emotional development of our students. There is also a need to focus on teaching the coping skills necessary to live in our rapidly changing world.

Some of the lessons in this book, such as *Self-Awareness*, *Peer Relationships/Friendship*, *Communication*, and *Goals/Organization* relate to the growth of the individual. Although they are included in various books and materials, they are important in the development of the whole child. Other topics, including *Anger/Conflict*, *Children of Divorce*, and *Grief and Loss* have also been dealt with, but there is a necessity for further information and new ways of presenting it to the students. Because these issues have become even more prevalent in society today, it is essential that we facilitate the knowledge and skills necessary to deal with these concerns.

We are living in a time of intolerance and transition that has escalated in scope. Bullying has reached new proportions that include cell phone texting and the internet. For this reason, the book delves into the issues of *Bullying/Harassment*, *Diversity/Tolerance*, and *Transition/Mobility*. We are surrounded by new fears of violence and terror brought about by intolerance and a lack of understanding about diversity. A rise in immigration brings with it the concerns of adjusting to environments filled with new cultures, customs, and languages. Chaos, escalating stresses, and anxieties bring forth a need for individuals to gain a sense of control in their lives. It is my purpose to deal with all of the rapidly growing concerns presented in this book.

There are a few reasons why I chose to write this book. I was a school counselor for over 23 years. Before that, I was a classroom teacher. As a counselor, I incorporated my teaching skills into educating children and adolescents concerning their own growth and development. I recently retired from the school system. During my last year at a K-8 center, there were over 1300 students with two counselors. With almost 700 students to service, individual counseling alone could not meet the needed demands. If I had been fortunate enough to have had 300, or even 200, students to service, I still would not have been able to effectively counsel each student on an individual basis.

There are a number of reasons that I have found classroom affective lessons and small group counseling to be beneficial in meeting the affective needs of my students. Today, with growing societal pressures and stresses, more and more children and adolescents are seeking counseling support. In classroom, or large group guidance, I was able to teach basic skills to all of the students that enhanced their growth and development. It also gave these students the opportunity to get to know me, and to better understand my role as their counselor.

Although large group affective lessons reach a greater number of students, smaller group counseling sessions are essential for students who have special needs. It offers an opportunity for these students to share similar concerns with each other. They begin to realize that others have similar problems and issues, and that it is not a "just me" situation. The students not only have an opportunity to share their thoughts and feelings with their peers, but also are able to discuss and process them as well.

It is generally in a small group setting that children and adolescents find a safe environment in which to release their thoughts and emotions. There are circumstances, however, where either students have difficulty discussing their issues among their peers, or are in more of a crisis situation. These are matters that are best served by individual counseling. The topics and lessons in this book may be modified or restructured to work with these students on an individual basis.

I have found excellent books and materials on group counseling over the years. However, I felt that there were areas that were essential to this day and time that needed to be addressed further, such as diversity and tolerance, transitions and mobility, and bullying and harassment. It was because of the relevance of these topics today, and the necessity to deal with them in a school setting, that this book was formulated.

As president of the Florida School Counselor Association, and the Florida Association for Specialists in Group Work, as well as elementary vice-president of the American School Counselor Association, I had the opportunity over the past few years to discuss counseling issues and concerns with other school counselors throughout the country. These occasions, as well as my own experiences as a school counselor for over two decades, were instrumental in my choosing what I thought to be the top 10 topics for counselors working with students in the school environment. Besides the three vital issues mentioned above, the other seven topics were chosen because they are so highly prevalent and relevant among our children and adolescents in the present day.

It is one thing to have books and materials available for school counselors to use in counseling their students, but it is of no value unless the counselor feels confident enough to actually facilitate small groups. Working as an adjunct professor in group counseling a number of years ago, I stressed the importance of small group counseling with my graduate students. I emphasized that the goal of the course was not only to teach group counseling skills, but also to instill an awareness of the value and effectiveness of group counseling in the school setting. I encouraged them to let go of their fears of small group counseling and incorporate it into their comprehensive school counseling program.

My purpose for writing this book is so that counselors might have a resource at hand that focuses on timely and critical issues in counseling children and adolescents. It is my hope that *Top 10 Topics for School Counselors* will offer school counselors lessons, discussion questions, and activities that will be helpful in working with their students in their own school settings. It is also my wish that this book will ease the pathway toward helping our students grow and develop into healthy, positive, productive, and self-fulfilled individuals.

HOW TO USE THIS BOOK

Top 10 Topics for School Counselors is written as a resource book for counselors to use with students in grades 3-8. It can be adapted, however, to other grades and particular situations according to the ages, abilities, and ethnicities of the students.

Following the Introduction, the book is divided into ten topics that deal with timely, critical issues prevalent with school children and adolescents in today's society. A brief description of these topics is presented below:

- *Self-Awareness* presents an opportunity for students to become more aware of themselves as individuals, as well as members of the societies in which they live.
- *Peer Relationships/Friendship* helps students discover how to relate to classmates and other students their age.
- *Communication* involves listening and responding to the thoughts and feelings of others, as well as having your own thoughts and feelings validated.
- *Anger/Conflict* aids students in learning to control and deal with anger and stress, and to resolve conflicts in a positive manner.
- *Bullying/Harassment* focuses on various types of bullying; explains the roles of the bully, victim, and bystander; and denotes ways of dealing with these issues.
- *Diversity/Tolerance* illustrates the importance of understanding the cultures, customs, and ethnicities of people from other countries and regions; accepting their similarities and differences; and standing up for the rights of all people.
- *Goals/Organization* leads students toward using time wisely and putting forth serious effort in preparing for short- and long-term goals.
- *Transition/Mobility* discusses the movement of students from country to country, state to state, city to city, and school to school. It also delves into the concerns of immigrant families and the stresses involved in their movement.

- *Children of Divorce* helps children and adolescents deal with the emotions and confusions of divorce and separation by helping to bring feelings out into the open.
- *Grief and Loss* explains the stages of grief, teaches coping skills, and helps students express the feelings they hide inside.

Each of the above issues begins with the purpose and objectives of that lesson. The session is presented with comprehensive directions for the counselor to follow. The seasoned counselors will be able to relate to these directions in terms of their present expertise, as well as benefit from new ideas. The novice counselors will be able to gain confidence with their ability to facilitate group counseling through the clear and concise presentations of the topics to the students. In many cases, a complete dialogue is available for the counselor's use in presenting the lessons and activities. These dialogues are written for the ease of the counselor in communicating the lessons to the students, but they can be modified with the counselor's own words and teaching/counseling styles.

The activities have been created to help the students gain a better understanding of the topics as the problems and concerns relate to them. It offers insight into the thoughts and feelings of the students as they learn to comprehend the issues and learn how to deal with them.

As significant as the presentations of the lessons and activities are, it's the dynamics of the discussion and processing of this exchange that is of most value. This is the stage where students gain the most awareness of their own issues and concerns and learn to process them in terms of themselves and their relationships with their peers. It cannot be emphasized enough that ample time must be given toward this discussion and processing period.

It is my hope that counselors will be better able to facilitate their group counseling sessions through the activities and discussion questions found in this book. It is important for them to be cognizant and knowledgeable of the topics, issues, and concerns that confront the children and adolescents who live in our ever-changing world, among our multicultural societies, volatile communities, and varying school environments.

1. SELF-AWARENESS

By becoming more aware of our thoughts, feelings, and actions, we learn more about the significance of self-confidence, mutual respect, and independence. The activities in this section focus on the following issues:

- Having pride in oneself is a form of dignity, value, and self-respect.
- Giving positive feedback to others, and receiving the same in return, helps to develop a stronger self-image.
- An attitude is a state of mind that involves one's thoughts and feelings and influences actions.

PRIDE BINGO

Purpose:
to increase a sense of self-awareness and pride

Objective:
Group members will gain an understanding of what it means to have pride in oneself.

Materials:
Pride Words List; paper bag; a copy of the blank *Pride Bingo* card for each student; colored construction paper to make paper "markers" to be used to cover words on the *Pride Bingo* cards during the activity (approximately 25 "markers" for each student)

Directions:
Having pride in oneself is a form of dignity, value, and self-respect. Feeling a sense of pride gives students satisfaction in their achievements, peer relationships, and self-worth. It also involves treating others the way they would like to be treated.

The Pride Bingo game includes words that are instrumental in developing a sense of pride and self-worth. Although the game in itself is fun, it is the meaning behind the activity that is valuable.

1. ***Pride Bingo cards*** - Make enough *Pride Bingo* cards so that each student in the class (or group) will be able to receive a card. Using the *Pride Words List*, write a word in each square on a Pride Bingo card, in the order they appear on the list, until all of the cards are filled with Pride Words. (When you get to the end of the list, start over with the first word and continue until all of the cards are complete. There are enough Pride Words so that no two cards will be exactly alike.)

2. ***"Markers"*** - Cut small squares of colored construction paper to use as "markers" during the game to cover the words.

3. ***Pride Words to be called out*** - Make a copy of the *Pride Words* page. Cut out each *Pride Word* separately, and place them all in a bag.

4. ***Pride Bingo Cards*** – Hand out one *Pride Bingo* card to each student. Pass out paper "markers" to be shared by group members. Have the group members cover the FREE space on their cards.

5. ***Playing the game*** - To begin the game of *Pride Bingo*, have the counselor or group leader, draw a word from the bag and call it out to the group members, either defining the word or using it in a sentence. When the student has the word on his or her card, he or she is to cover it with a paper marker. When a student covers a column or row with their markers, he or she calls out *Pride Bingo* and wins that game. (You may add the diagonal rows, if you choose.) Each winner calls out the words that are in his or her winning column or row, checking them with the counselor or group leader. If they are correct, you may want to give winners a prize, i.e., a sticker *(optional)*.

Note to Counselors: You may wish to collect all materials (the *Pride Bingo* cards, "markers," and bag of *Pride Words*) after each lesson to use for future classes or groups.

Discussion Questions:

1. What did you learn from this activity?
2. Why is the meaning behind the *Pride Bingo* game more important than the activity itself?
3. What are some of the words that are most important to you?
4. Tell about a time when you were caring, helpful, loyal, or any other of the *Pride Words*.
5. Tell of a time you felt pride in yourself for something you accomplished.
6. If you looked in a mirror, which words would appear as a reflection of you?
7. Why is it important to feel a sense of pride or self-worth?

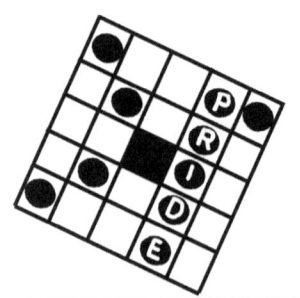

PRIDE WORDS LIST

NICE	HARD-WORKING	PATIENT	DEPENDABLE
KIND	RELIABLE	ENTHUSIASTIC	JOVIAL
THOUGHTFUL	FAITHFUL	PERSEVERING	ATTENTIVE
HELPFUL	UNSELFISH	TOLERANT	POLITE
RESPECTFUL	GOOD SPORT	CONSIDERATE	EAGER
COMMITTED	PLEASANT	EMPATHIC	RELAXED
PROUD	SUPPORTIVE	DETERMINED	UNSELFISH
COOPERATIVE	STRONG-MINDED	ORGANIZED	APPRECIATIVE
CARING	AFFECTIONATE	LOYAL	GENEROUS
SWEET	FORGIVING	CHEERFUL	GENTLE
FOCUSED	ACTIVE	FLEXIBLE	GIVING
CURIOUS	INDUSTRIOUS	CONSCIENTIOUS	HAPPY
THANKFUL	CONTENTED	LOVING	SYMPATHETIC
RESPONSIBLE	COMPLIMENTARY	COURAGEOUS	STUDIOUS
COURTEOUS	USEFUL	PRODUCTIVE	TRUTHFUL
DILIGENT	HONEST	REFLECTIVE	INQUISITIVE
GRATEFUL	PATRIOTIC	FUNNY	CAPABLE
SENSE OF HUMOR	LIKEABLE	CONFIDENT	EXUBERANT
BIG-HEARTED	FUN	TRUSTWORTHY	POSITIVE ATTITUDE

PRIDE BINGO

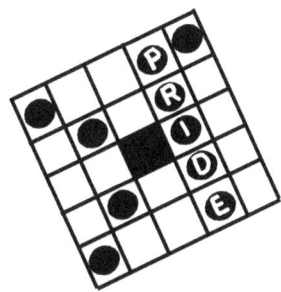

SELF-PORTRAIT

Purpose:
to increase self-awareness and gain acceptance and pride

Objective:
Group members will receive positive feedback from each other through the use of positive messages.

Materials:
a copy of the activity page, *Self-Portrait*, for each student; pencils; crayons and/or colored markers

Directions/Activity:
It is important to feel important and to help others feel the same way. Sometimes, just a kind word or positive message that you extend to someone else makes a difference in the way they feel or view themselves. Giving positive feedback to others, and receiving the same in return, helps to develop a stronger self-image and a feeling of pride. The following activity helps students reach this goal.

Tell the students to close their eyes and focus on something negative. After a short time, tell them to open their eyes. Ask them, "How do you feel?" After a few minutes of discussion, instruct them to close their eyes again. This time tell them to focus on something positive. Examples might be: *a day at the beach, hitting the ball when it's your turn at bat, riding a bike with your friend, or getting a good grade on a test that you studied for.* After a moment, have the students open their eyes. Ask them, "How do you feel now?" "Why do you think it is important to feel positive and help others feel the same way?"

Form a circle (or circles if in a classroom) of 6-8 students. Give out a copy of the *Self Portrait* activity page to each student. Instruct your students to put their name at the top of the paper. Next, give the students about 5-6 minutes to draw their self-portraits. When they are finished, have them pass their papers to the person on their right. These students will then write something **positive** about the person whose name is on the top of the paper. (Emphasize the word "positive"). Circulate among the students to make sure that the words stay positive. Every 30 seconds, have the students pass their papers to the right and follow the same procedure until the paper gets back to the original owner. Give the students a few moments to read the positive messages on their papers. Offer students an opportunity to share one or two messages that they especially like with the whole group. Have the students take the *Self-Portrait* home with them and tape it to their mirror. Tell them that they should read the positive messages at least once each day.

Discussion Questions:

1. What did you learn from this activity?
2. How did it feel to give a positive message?
3. How did it feel to receive a positive message?
4. Which was more difficult: giving or receiving a positive message?
5. How did it feel to share a positive message with the whole group?
6. How did this activity help you increase self-awareness or gain a sense of acceptance and pride?

Alternative Activity:

Materials:

small pieces of paper, box or bag, pencils

Directions:

It feels good to be "in the spotlight" when receiving positive messages from others. Ask group members to sit in a circle. Have each student write his or her name on a small piece of paper and drop it in a designated box or bag. As group leader, draw one name and tell that person that he or she is "in the spotlight." The other group members are to go around the circle giving a positive message to that person. Examples might be: *You are a nice person. You are helpful to other people. I like your smile. You are a good reader.* The person who is "in the spotlight" is to answer with a simple, "thank you." The person who is giving the positive message must use eye contact and be genuine (real).

Additional Discussion Questions:

1. How did it feel to be "in the spotlight" and hear positive messages?
2. What difference do you think it would make in a school setting if students gave each other positive messages rather than negative messages?
3. How could you use positive messages at home as well as at school?

Self-Portrait

Name _____

ATTITUDE: A State of Mind

Purpose:

to help students become aware of their attitude and how it affects their thoughts and actions

Objective:

Students will become more aware of their attitude and how it affects what they think and what they do; they will more clearly understand that they can control their own attitudes.

Materials:

a copy of the activity page, *Check Out Your Attitude!* for each student

Directions:

An attitude is a state of mind, or a way of thinking, in a given situation. It involves your thoughts and feelings, and influences your actions. People who have positive attitudes usually show enthusiasm and interest in themselves and others. They enjoy learning and are able to work together with others. Their sense of humor helps them see the lighter side of situations and be open to change.

People who have negative attitudes wake up in the morning thinking it's going to be a miserable day. They often do not work well with others because their thinking leads them to find fault and place blame. They usually are not very considerate or caring. People with negative attitudes generally feel things are just too much trouble, or that it doesn't really matter.

Doors of opportunity open up to people with positive outlooks on life. They typically feel better about themselves and aren't afraid of making mistakes. They set goals and work to achieve them. They don't give up when the going's rough. In treating others the way they want to be treated, people with positive attitudes gain a sense of respect and caring. By being open-minded, they are prepared for new ideas and accept change.

This lesson is meant to help students become more aware of their own attitudes, and to determine whether their general approach to life is positive or negative.

Discuss the information concerning positive and negative attitudes with the students. The comments and questions listed below will help facilitate the discussion:

- "Attitude is a state of mind." What do you think that means? How can it influence your actions?
- In what ways do people with positive attitudes display their thoughts, feelings, and actions?
- How do people with negative attitudes typically wake up in the morning? How would you describe the way they usually think and/or act?
- What do you think is meant by the expression, "doors of opportunity?"
- How would you explain what is meant by a "positive outlook on life?"
- In what ways are "doors of opportunity open to people with positive outlooks on life?

The following activity will assist students in learning not only about their own attitudes, but how they can go about being in control of their thoughts, feelings, and actions.

Hand out a copy of the activity page, *Check Out Your Attitude!* to each student. Begin the lesson by saying: *We have just discussed the differences between positive and negative attitudes, or ways of thinking, feeling, and acting. Have you ever thought about your own attitude? What is it like? Is it generally positive or negative? Step outside yourself and take a good look at yourself. How do you think others would describe your attitude?*

You are about to "check out your attitude" by completing the positive attitude checklist in front of you. This checklist is for you. It will not be handed in. It is a means for you to think about how you typically think, feel, or act in various situations. If you are honest with yourself when you answer the questions, you will be more aware of whether you have a positive or negative outlook on life. Whatever the outcome of the checklist, you are in control of attitude and how it affects what you think and feel and do.

As you work through the activity page, read each question carefully, and then check either "yes" or "no" to the question asked. You will be given about 8-10 minutes to finish the exercise. If you are through before then, wait patiently for the other students to finish.

Discussion Questions:

1. How did you feel as you answered the questions on the checklist?
2. Did you find it a positive or negative experience?
3. Look over your checklist. Pick out five situations that best describe you or your attitude, and put a star in front of them. Would anyone like to share the situations that you selected with the whole group?
4. Why do you think that being a good listener would demonstrate a positive attitude?
5. Why would a person who works well with others have a positive attitude?
6. Picture a person in your mind whom you think generally has a positive attitude. Without naming names, who would like to describe the characteristics of that person?
7. Why would a person with a positive outlook on life probably be more successful in his or her life than a person with a negative attitude.
8. A person with a positive attitude "believes in himself or herself." What do you think is meant by that statement?
9. Do you think a person with a positive way of thinking would get more enjoyment out of life than a person who thinks and acts in a negative manner?
10. Why are you in control of your attitude? What can you do to change negative thoughts and actions into a more positive approach to life?

 # CHECK OUT YOUR ATTITUDE

	YES	NO
1. Are you considerate of others?	___	___
2. Are you usually enthusiastic in what you say and do?	___	___
3. Do you work well with others?	___	___
4. Do you listen to others and learn from them?	___	___
5. Do you have a sense of humor?	___	___
6. Are you helpful and considerate?	___	___
7. Do you wake up with a good feeling about the day?	___	___
8. Do you set goals and try to accomplish them?	___	___
9. Are you polite and respectful toward others?	___	___
10. Are you on time for school and for your classes?	___	___
11. Do you do your homework without grumbling?	___	___
12. Do you respect the rights of others?	___	___
13. Do you try to learn from your mistakes?	___	___
14. Do you always put forth your best effort?	___	___
15. Do you try to make the best of situations?	___	___
16. Do you usually wear a smile on your face?	___	___
17. Do you make friends – and keep friends?	___	___
18. Are you proud of who you are?	___	___

2. PEER RELATIONSHIPS

These years are critical in the development of healthy relationships. The activities in this section focus on the following issues:

- Some people dwell on the negative rather than the positive aspects of themselves and others.
- People usually look at the behaviors of others and pass judgment according to these behaviors.
- If a person says, "Nobody likes me," the answer might be, "Maybe they just don't know you!"

COMPLIMENT BAG

Purpose:

to be able to develop awareness of self and others by giving and receiving compliments and affirmative messages

Objective:

Students will be able to give themselves complimentary or affirmative messages, and be able to receive compliments graciously from others.

Materials:

small, lunch-sized bags (one for each student and one for the group leader); strips of paper (three for each student and three for the leader); pencils or pens; crayons or colored markers

Materials:

Some people dwell on the negative rather than the positive aspects of themselves and others. People who do give compliments to others may have difficulty accepting compliments when the affirmative messages are directed at them. If a person tells someone he or she likes his or her shirt or dress, it isn't unusual for the person to respond with, "Oh, this old thing? I just found it in my closet!" Sometimes it is more difficult to receive compliments than to give them.

The following activity, *Compliment Bag*, is directed toward not only learning to give compliments, but also learning to receive them graciously, as well. The students will learn that when they receive a compliment they should respond with two special words, "thank you," and allow themselves to enjoy the warmth of the compliment.

To start the activity, give each student a paper bag and crayons, or colored markers. (They may have their own crayons or markers, or may share with other students in the group). Instruct the students as follows: *Decorate your bag with a picture of a place that is special for you, and then print your name at the top of the bag.*

Next, give each student three strips of paper. Ask them to: *write a compliment that you would enjoy hearing about yourself from others. Write a different compliment on each strip of paper. When you are through writing, fold each strip of paper twice, and then put the three folded strips into your paper bag.* To get the compliment writing process started, give some examples that perhaps you might like to hear from others

Tell the students you will give them directions on what they will be doing next, but they are to wait for you to give the signal before starting. Give them the following directions: *Walk around the room holding your open bag in front of you. Approach another student, reach into his or her bag and pull out a folded strip of paper. Open the paper, say the person's name, and read the compliment.* **Make sure you are genuine; read it with meaning.** *The person's reply should be "thank you." Next, that person will reach into your bag and return the favor. Try choosing a kid you don't know very well.* Remind the students to put the compliment strip back into the bag after it is read.

Allow about 5-6 minutes for this activity. Then, stop the action, and say: *If there is a compliment that you aren't hearing enough, or at all, take the other two compliments out of the bag and just leave in the one you want to hear.*

After allowing approximately 2-3 minutes for the students to read their special compliment to each other, signal the students that the activity is over and have them return to their seats. Tell the students that when they are at home and feel they need to hear some complimentary words, or want to have a need met, to use the "complimentary bag" with a family member or friend. For example, they could write: *"I could use a hug!" "I don't tell you often enough, but you are special to me." " Thank you for being a good friend." "You are a helpful person."*

Discussion Questions:

1. Why do you think you were asked to draw a picture on your bag of a place that is special to you? Is it telling something positive about you? How does it make you feel to look at this picture? How does it feel to give a compliment?

2. How does it feel to receive a compliment, especially one you like to hear?

3. Is it easier to give a compliment or receive one?

4. Why is it important to be genuine when you give a compliment? Will the other person know if you aren't being genuine, or real?

5. Why is it sometimes best to just say "thank you" as a reply to a compliment?

6. What have you learned from this activity that will be helpful to you in the future?

Alternative Activity

Materials:

one sheet of paper and a pencil for each student

Directions:

You might want to call this activity, *Give Yourself A Hand*.

It is a way to "pat yourself on the back." Give a sheet of paper and a pencil to each student. Ask the students to trace one of their hands on the piece of paper, and then write their name at the top. When you give the signal to start, they are to walk around the room and exchange their paper with another student. Each student will write a compliment inside the other student's hand outline. The students will then give the papers back to their owners, saying a simple "thank you", and then choose another student with whom to exchange papers. Repeat the process, moving around the room changing partners for about 8-10 minutes. Remind students that the lesson is on compliments or statements, not negative statements.

After the allotted period of time, or when you feel it is time to stop, ask the students to return to their desks. Give them a few minutes to read the compliments on their "hand" to themselves. Ask the students to choose a compliment that is especially meaningful to them. Allow those students who wish to share with the whole group to do so.

Additional Discussion Questions:

1. Why do you think this activity is called "Give Yourself A Hand?"
2. How does it feel to receive compliments from your peers?
3. How does it feel to give a compliment to someone else?
4. Even if you don't know someone well, or he or she isn't really a close friend, can you find something good to say about that person?
5. How did it feel to share one of the compliments you received with the whole group?
6. What is something new you learned from this activity?

Suggestion: Propose to students: Take your "hand" home and tape it to a wall or mirror so that you can read the compliments to yourself each day. This is especially great to do on days that your self-image could use a boost.

IS YOUR BEHAVIOR REALLY YOU?

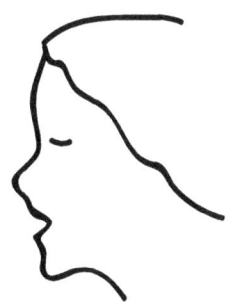

Purpose:

to help students visualize their behaviors and how they may be viewed by their peers

Objective:

Students will gain a better understanding of their own behaviors and how those behaviors may affect their relationships with their peers.

Materials:

a copy of the activity page, *Actions Speak Louder than Words*, for each student; whiteboard or flipchart

Directions:

We probably all know students who clown around in class. We also can visualize students who threaten other students or call them names. What about those students who try to hide and act very quiet so that no one calls on them? Can you think of any students you have worked with who give up without really trying when it comes to schoolwork or homework? We all have seen students who display these types of behaviors. Generally, a sense of wanting to belong leads to certain misbehaviors that serve a purpose, whether it's gaining attention, feeling a sense of power, lashing out in revenge, or giving up. These negative behaviors cause even further feelings of frustration and confusion because they push people away from them, not towards them.

The following activity can help children to recognize the effects of both positive and negative behaviors. To introduce this lesson to the students, say the following: *People usually look at the behaviors of others and pass judgment according to these behaviors. Although it's easy to see the behaviors of others, it's important to be able to look at our own behaviors, as well. We need to take notice of how we act and how we come across to others. We need to take a look at what messages we are sending. Does your behavior draw people to you or push them away? Do you make friends easily and keep them as friends? Do you feel you belong, or do you feel "left out?"*

Before passing out the activity page to the students, write the following words on the whiteboard or flipchart and discuss their meanings as defined below:

- *Attention* – a need to be looked at, listened to, or cared about
- *Power* – a need for strength or control
- *Revenge* – a need to get even, pay back, or gain satisfaction for a wrong or injury
- *Giving up* – not trying because of fear of failure or concern about being able to succeed

Leave these words and their definitions on the board as a source of reference for the students as they work through the activity page.

Hand out the *Actions Speak Louder Than Words* activity page. (Tell the students that the names used in this activity are picked at random with no one person in mind.) Emphasize that it is important that the students take a look at **themselves** and not point out or criticize others. Ask them to see if they recognize any of the characters in themselves.

Give the following instructions to the students: *In the space provided under each story, write the purpose, or reason, for the negative behavior: Attention, Power, Revenge, or Giving up. If you feel the story does not show negative behavior, write "Positive behavior" under it. Fill in your answers by using the words in the Key at the top of the page. Use the definitions on the board for reference as you do your work.*

Allow approximately 10-12 minutes to complete the activity. Next, call on one student at a time to read a story. Then, have the student relate what he or she wrote as the purpose, or reason, for the behavior in the story. After all of the stories have been read, go over the discussion questions with the group or class.

Is Your Behavior Really You? Answer Key:

Bobby Butt-In, *Power*; Corey Comedian, *Attention*; Wanda Who? *Giving up*; Charlie Cheerful, *Positive behavior*; Serina Secrets, *Revenge*; Billy Bully, *Power*; Connie Compliment, *Positive behavior*; Carey Critical, *Power*; Nina Know-It-All, *Attention*; Casey Can't, *Giving up*

Alternative Activities

- Have the students role-play the various characters from the Actions Speak Louder Than Words activity page.

Note to Counselors: It is easier to look at negative behaviors than positive ones, however, it's important to **emphasize** positive behaviors with the students. Some alternative discussions might be:

- List the characters with misbehaviors (from the Actions Speak Louder Than

Words activity page) on the board or flipchart. Ask the students what they might say to each of these "characters" to help them change their negative behaviors to positive behaviors.

- Ask the students to see if they can think of any other positive behaviors that might enhance, or improve, peer relationships, for example: kindness, thoughtfulness, honesty, loyalty, respect, etc.:

Discussion Questions:

1. What do you think that "Bobby Butt-In" gains from his actions? Do you think this is a good way to make friends?

2. Do you think people laugh with or laugh at "Corey Comedian?" What is the difference?

3. By being so quiet, what do you think that "Wanda Who?" misses out on?

4. Do you think that if "Serena Secret" tells you about someone else when she is upset with him or her, that she would tell secrets about you when she was upset with you? Can you trust her?

5. Have you ever felt that you were being bullied by someone like "Billy Bully?" Without naming names or pointing fingers, tell about a time someone bullied you.

6. What might you say to "Carey Critical" if he constantly criticized your friend about what he/she wore or what he/she said? What might you say if the critical remarks were made toward you?

7. If you had a friend or acquaintance that was a "Nina Know-It-All," how would it make you feel?

8. "Casey Can't" feels that she isn't capable of succeeding in or out of school. What do you think is meant by the statement, "Those who do not try, do not fail?"

9. What do you think that "Charlie Cheerful" and "Connie Compliment" have in common? Do you think they have many friends? Why?

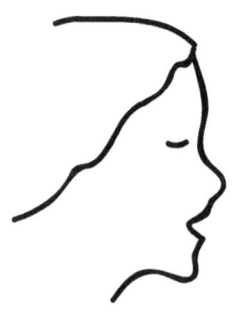

ACTIONS SPEAK LOUDER THAN WORDS

Key: *Attention   Power   Revenge   Giving up   Positive behavior*

Bobby Butt-In always tries to push his way in the front of the line whether it is at lunch, at the water fountain, or on the playground. Sometimes, it leads to pushing and shoving by the students around him. One time, a student behind him fell and skinned his knee.

Purpose, or reason, for behavior _____

Corey Comedian has a great sense of humor and gains lots of laughs from the other students. Sometimes the humor is appropriate, but often times it is during class when the teacher is teaching, a student is answering a question or giving a report, or when the class is busy doing their assignments.

Purpose, or reason, for behavior _____

Wanda Who? is a very quiet girl who sits in the back of the classroom. She doesn't feel that she is very smart, so she doesn't raise her hand to answer questions. She most certainly doesn't make any eye contact with the teacher. She doesn't really talk to the other students in the class since she feels they probably wouldn't like her anyway. She feels it's just no use.

Purpose, or reason, for behavior _____

Charlie Cheerful enters the classroom with a smile and big "hello" for those around him. He looks forward to the day of learning, as well as the social times with his friends. He makes and keeps friends easily.

Purpose, or reason, for behavior _____

Serena Secrets usually has something to say about others. When she is upset with another student, she will usually tell "secrets" about them, sometimes starting untrue rumors. She often has problems keeping friends.

Purpose, or reason, for behavior _____

ACTIONS SPEAK LOUDER THAN WORDS
Page 2

Billy Bully thinks he's tough! He makes fun of other students in his class, often calling them names or embarrassing them with his comments. He tries to trip students when they walk by his desk, and sometimes threaten them when they say they are going to report him. Most of his friends are just like him. Others may *say* they are his friends because they are afraid of him.

Purpose, or reason, for behavior _____

Connie Compliment always seems to have a kind word or comment for the other students. She is genuine, or real, in what she says. Often the flattering remarks she gives to others brightens their day. She always seems to see the best in people.

Purpose, or reason, for behavior _____

Carey Critical has no trouble finding fault with others, whether it's the way they talk, the clothes they wear, what they do, or what they say. Generally, he finds fault with others, but never with himself.

Purpose, or reason, for behavior _____

Nina Know-It-All has the answer before others even get a chance to reply. No matter what others may think or feel, she is always right. Even when she doesn't know an answer, or even the topic, she will put her two-cents in anyway! For what it's worth, she *always* knows best.

Purpose, or reason, for behavior _____

Casey Can't never feels she is capable of doing what others do. In the classroom, she looks at the directions on an assignment and decides she can't do it even before she begins the first problem. During P.E. class, she doesn't even attempt to hit the softball, because she *knows* she's can't do it.

Purpose, or reason, for behavior _____

NOBODY LIKES ME: Maybe They Just Don't Know You!

Purpose:

to offer students the possibility of making new friends by giving them the opportunity to get to know each other better

Objective:

Students will be able to develop new friendships by discovering each other's likes, interests, dreams, goals, etc.

Materials:

large construction paper (one sheet for each student); picture magazines, scissors, glue or glue sticks, crayons or colored markers

Directions:

Nobody likes me! How many times have we heard that comment from students who come into the counselor's office, or meet the counselor in the hallways? When I hear those words from a student who is "down and out," my answer is often *"maybe they just don't know you!"* When Jane came into my office one day near the middle of the school year, we went through that same dialogue. After talking to her for a while to see what she was thinking, and how she was feeling, I suggested that, with her help, we would form a small group to make new friends. I asked her to name three students in her classroom whom she would like to get to know better. I told her that the three other students would not know that she had given me their names.

The next day, I called all four students down to my office. I told them that sometimes I get a small group together just to get to know them better. I then asked them if they would like to do an activity together called *All About Me Collage*. They agreed (they always do!), so I welcomed them to our small group setting, telling them that we would meet that day, and then again for one more session. (I gave them the date and time).

During the second session, when a student talked about his or her collage, another student would give a comment, such as: "I like the same thing!" or, "I have a dog, too!" With all their chatting during the activity, they soon became friends. Following the group sessions, I checked with Jane to see if her situation had changed. She told me that she now had friends. Her new friends were given the chance to get to know her, just as she took advantage of the opportunity to get to know them.

The "All About Me" Collage activity is facilitated in two sessions. (See Session #1 and Session #2 below) If time does not permit two sessions, there is a choice of two alternative activities that can be completed in only one session.

"All About Me" Collage, Session #1 (30 minutes)

The students are asked to sit in a circle. In the middle of the circle, place a number of colorful picture magazines, scissors, and glue or glue sticks. Then introduce the activity to the students: *I would like to get to know you better, and at the same time, you will all get to know each other better, too. I am giving each of you a sheet of construction paper. In the center of the circle are magazines, scissors, and glue (or glue stick). What I would like for you to do during the next 20 minutes is to cut out pictures and words from the magazines that tell about you . . . how you picture yourself, your likes, interests, hobbies; your family and pets; your dreams and goals in school and outside of school. Glue these onto the construction paper that is in front of you. Make sure to put your name on the paper.*

Facilitate the students along the way. Talk about the pictures they are cutting out. Remind them to look for different kinds of pictures that tell about them. Tell them that if they see something in a magazine that they think perhaps one of the other students may be able to use, offer it to him or her. If they are looking for a certain kind of picture, tell them to let the others know. Maybe they could help each other. Listen to the conversation among the students as they work, and watch their non-verbal language to see how they are interacting. Guide them toward finishing their collages within the 20-minute time frame.

After the allotted time, tell the students: *You have been creating your collages during the past 20 minutes and they are looking great! I am going to collect the collages and hold them until the next session, (date/time). During that session, you will all share your "All About Me Collages" with each other. I'm looking forward to getting to learn more about each of you, as well.*

"All About Me" Collage, Session #2 (30 minutes)

Ask the students to sit in a circle. Give them the following instructions: *I am giving you the collages you created during the session on (day of first session). Each of you will have the opportunity to share your "All About Me Collage" with the group. Through learning about each other's likes, interests and hobbies; families and pets; and dreams and goals in school and outside of school, you will be allowing others to get to know you better. Who would like to be the first to share?*

After each student describes his or her collage to the group, allow a few minutes for the other students to ask a question or share a comment. Be sure to facilitate in a way that each student has equal time to share with the group. The sharing session should take approximately 20 minutes. Use the last 10 minutes of the group session to talk about the "Discussion Questions" written that follow.

Discussion Questions:

1. What have you learned about yourself from creating the "All About Me" Collage?
2. What have you learned about the other students in your group?
3. Does everyone have the same likes, interests, family members, pets, or goals? Do you think that is okay? Why?
4. Do you feel you know each other better than you did when you started the group? In what ways? How is that helpful in forming new friendships?
5. Can people still be friends even if they have different interests, etc.?
6. Would you recommend this type of "getting to know you" group to other students?

Alternative Activity: (one-session)

Materials:

a copy of the activity page, *"ME" Collage*, or a copy of the activity page, *"I" Collage*, for each student

Directions:

Instead of using a sheet of construction paper and magazines, give a copy of either the *"ME" Collage* activity page or the *"I" Collage* activity page to the students. Ask them the following: What interests do you have at home and at school? Who are the members of your family? What are your favorite hobbies, foods, books, etc.? Write a different word or phrase about yourself in each puzzle piece. You may also draw a picture, if you choose

After about 15-20 minutes, culminate the activity with one of the following:

7. Have the students share their collages with the whole group (one person at a time) and explain what they wrote (or drew) that tells about themselves.
8. Have the students cut out their puzzle pieces. Put the students into pairs, and have the partners exchange their puzzle pieces. Each student will put together his or her partner's puzzle pieces. When everyone is finished putting the puzzles together, the students will sit behind their own puzzles. They will then take turns describing what the words and drawings tell about them.

"ME" COLLAGE

"I" Collage

3. COMMUNICATION

Since we all have our own perceptions and interpretations, communication takes place only when one person understands what the other person means by what he or she is saying. The activities in this section focus on the following:

- In working toward a cooperative goal, students need to be able to perceive or view ideas from different perspectives.
- Use of listening skills, as well as concentration, is necessary in performing tasks that involve following directions.
- The way people portray themselves to others directly impacts the way they are treated in return.

GROUP STORY

Purpose:

to use communication skills toward developing a diversity of ideas in a cooperative manner

Objective:

Students will be able to create a story through cooperative input from each group member.

Materials:

whiteboard or flipchart, pen

Directions/Activity:

Sometimes we get stuck seeing things from only one perspective – our own. Communication skills include the art of being able to perceive or view ideas from different perspectives. We need to be open to other people's thoughts and visions, as well as our own.

The following activity allows us to see how change occurs when we allow ourselves to use a diversity of ideas to write a story. Through group effort, students will develop a story in a cooperative manner.

Have students decide on a topic or theme for their story by brainstorming ideas. The counselor or group leader will write down all of the ideas on the board or flipchart. The students will then vote on one idea to use as the topic or theme.

If the students are in a small group setting, have them sit in a circle. Choose one student to begin the cooperative story by giving an opening sentence. The counselor or group leader will then write this sentence on the board or flipchart.

One student at a time will go around the circle (or the room, if it is a large group) and add a sentence to the story until everyone has an opportunity to contribute. In a small group setting, it may be feasible to go around the circle twice. The last student will give a closing sentence. The counselor or group leader can guide the course of the story by asking, "What happened next? Why, how, where, when did it occur? How does it end?" Etc. The counselor or facilitator will write all of the sentences on the board or flipchart from beginning to end.

At the end of the group session, the counselor or group leader will read the story back to the students, emphasizing how the story was a group effort using a diversity of ideas that involved working together in a cooperative manner.

(Optional) Each student may wish to copy the story, highlighting the part(s) he or she contributed, and take the lesson home to share with his or her family.

Discussion Questions:

1. How difficult was it to come to an agreement on a topic or theme for the story?
2. Did everyone get the topic or theme he or she wanted?
3. Did the story turn out differently than you expected at the beginning?
4. How did you feel about sharing the story with other group members? Did it make it more interesting?
5. What made this a "cooperative story"?
6. What might have happened if group members didn't cooperate?
7. How do you feel about writing a cooperative story? Would you rather write a story by yourself? Why, or why not?
8. What did you learn from this activity?

LISTENING SKILLS

Purpose:

to help students develop effective listening skills to be better able to follow directions

Objective:

Students will gain a better understanding of the need to listen and concentrate when given a task that involves following directions.

Materials:

none (If the first *Variations* activity is selected, students may use their own notebook paper).

Directions/Activity:

Use of listening skills, as well as concentration, is necessary in performing a task that involves following directions. When there is a list of directions given, memory also becomes an important factor. In the following activity, students will use listening skills and memory to recall details needed to follow directions.

Choose a different volunteer student for each of the tasks below. Give the specific directions to the student (as written below), telling him or her of the need to follow all of the directions **in the order they are given**. All directions are to be given before the student begins. Tell the students that the directions will be read **only one time,** so they must concentrate and listen carefully. Suggest to the students that it may be helpful to picture the details of the directions as they are given in order to complete the task.

Directions

1. Skip to the front door; turn the lights off and then back on; walk to the back of the room and bow; skip back to your seat.
2. Walk to the back of the room; do four jumping jacks; turn around twice; skip back to your seat.
3. Walk to the teacher's desk; sit down in the chair; stand up and push the chair under the desk; hop back to your seat.

4. Skip to the board; write your first and last names; say your full name out loud; hop back to your seat.

5. Turn around clockwise; turn around counterclockwise; jump up and down twice; skip back to your seat.

Variations:

Have the students write a set of four directions (Give examples similar to the directions given previously). Choose two volunteers to come to the front of the class. Have one of the students read his or her set of directions to the other student who will follow the directions in the order they are given. The students may then switch roles. After these students are seated, choose two more volunteers and continue in the same manner.

After demonstrating one or two of the *Directions* given in 1-5 on the previous page, choose two volunteers to come to the front of the class. Ask one student to make up a set of directions and tell them to the other student, who will follow the directions in the order given. (These directions will not be written). The students may then switch roles. After these students are seated, choose two more volunteers and continue in the same manner.

Discussion Questions:

1. How did it feel to have to listen and follow directions as they were given?

2. Did you feel confident or confused?

3. Did you have to concentrate?

4. How did you feel giving directions? Do you think it would be easier writing the directions first, or thinking them up in your head in the front of the class?

5. In what way did memory play a part in following directions?

6. In what way did you have to recall facts in order to follow the directions as given?

7. Why do you think it important to be able to listen and follow directions?

 WHAT IS THAT LABEL YOU ARE WEARING?

Purpose:
to demonstrate how "labels" are ways of communicating how you portray yourself or how others might view you

Objective:
Students will be able to recognize various "labels" that people wear and become more aware of not only how they may perceive themselves, but how others may view them, as well.

Materials:
one copy of the activity page, *Communicating Through Labels,* paper bag; adhesive or masking tape

Directions:
As a counselor, have you ever asked yourself why people are treated the way they are by others? If they are treated in a positive manner, there is no problem, but if they are treated in a negative way, it just doesn't feel very good. How often do people stop to look at themselves and take stock of what messages they are sending out to others around them? This lesson helps students understand that the way they portray themselves to others directly impacts the way they are treated in return.

Introduce this activity by explaining the following to the students: *Through both verbal and non-verbal communication, words, looks, gestures, posture, and expressions often give others the incentive, or reason, to label us, i.e., silly, grumpy, angry, unhappy, irritating, tattle tale, lazy, stupid, dishonest, liar, gossip, or bully. Positive labels may also be communicated, i.e., caring, cheerful, helpful, smart, honest, friendly, responsible, or loyal. Did you ever feel like you had a neon sign on your forehead that blinked: "I like myself" or "I don't like myself?" Or perhaps your neon sign is blinking: "Like me" or "Don't like me."*

Although words can lead toward communicating the way you are viewed by others, many times actions can speak louder than words. For instance, Julie is walking along, hanging her head, dragging her feet. You say, "Hi, Julie. How are you doing?" Julie answers, "Fine." Do you believe Julie's words or her actions?

Students often treat others the way they "ask" to be treated by the neon sign, or label, that they wear. The following activity, Communicating Through Labels helps students understand how wearing a "label" affects the way others treat them. (If you are working with a younger group of students, it would be helpful to explain the negative and positive "label words" to the children before beginning the activity).

1. Cut out the labels on the Communicating Through Labels activity page. Fold them in half and place them in a paper bag

2. If you are in a large group or classroom setting, select 20 students as participants. The rest of the class will be observers. Have each student draw a label out of the bag. Without letting the student see the label, tape it to his or her forehead. Continue this process until each of the selected students has a label taped to his or her forehead. (If you are in a small group setting, you will need as many labels as there are group members. Choose appropriate labels for your group's situation, or design new labels, if necessary.)

3. Instruct the students as follows: When I tell you to begin, you will move around the room. You will not know the label that is taped to your forehead. As you walk around, you will treat each other the way each person is labeled without saying the labeled word. For example: If Larry is wearing a label that says "angry," everyone will talk to him or treat him as though he were an angry person (without using the word "angry"). Larry must then try to guess what word is taped to his forehead, (It must be the exact word). If he guesses the word, he will continue walking around the room, interacting with other participants and continuing the activity.

4. The students who are acting as "observers" will watch the interactions among the participants. They will give their observations during the discussion period that follows the activity.

5. Allow approximately 8-10 minutes for the participants to guess their labels. (If at that time any of the participants have not been able to figure out their labels, the other participants can give bigger and bigger hints until these participants make the correct guess).

Discussion Questions:

Participants:

1. How did it feel to have a negative label? A positive label?
2. Was it easier to act out another person's label or guess your own?
3. Was there a point where you felt frustrated? Confused? Rejected?
4. What did you learn from this activity?

Observers:

1. What did you observe that was happening in this activity?
2. What did you observe about the participants who were acting out another person's label?
3. What did you observe about the person who was trying to guess his or her label?
4. What did you learn from this activity?

Everyone:

1. What part does "labeling" play in communicating information about yourself to others?
2. How can you change negative labels into positive ones?

 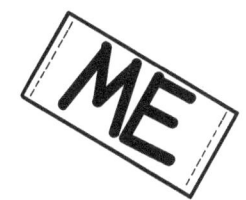

Communicating Through Labels

(Label Cut-outs)

SILLY	GRUMPY
ANGRY	UNHAPPY
TATTLE TALE	IRRITATING
LAZY	DISHONEST
LIAR	BULLY
GOSSIP	STUPID
CARING	CHEERFUL
HELPFUL	HONEST
FRIENDLY	LOYAL
SMART	RESPONSIBLE

4. ANGER/CONFLICT

The ability to control and manage feelings and behaviors is imperative in dealing with the conflict, pressure, and tension that have become part of our normal lives. The activities in this section focus on the following:

- Students need to learn how to respond appropriately to their own conflicts and take responsibility for helping to resolve their own problems.
- Understanding intensities of anger may help students recognize signs of frustration before they become overwhelming.
- Learning positive ways of reducing stress or tension will help students deal with pressure or conflict.

WHEN ONE DOOR CLOSES, ANOTHER ONE OPENS
Resolving Conflicts

Purpose:

to learn to deal with conflicts or problems

Objective:

Students will learn various strategies toward resolving conflicts, as well as gain an understanding of how and when to use them.

Materials:

a copy of the activity page, *Strategies to Resolve Conflicts*, for each student; a copy of the activity page, *Chosen Strategy*, for each student; whiteboard or flipchart

Directions:

There are various kinds of behaviors that people use to resolve their conflicts. It is important for students to learn the skills that accompany creative conflict resolution. Disagreements, arguments, and fights occur inside and outside of the classroom. It's not enough for teachers to be the peacemakers. Students need to learn to be peacemakers, as well. They need to be able to respond to their own conflicts and take responsibility for helping to resolve their own problems.

This lesson helps students to develop techniques for working through their conflicts. Sometimes situations can become worse, or more confusing, when everyone involved becomes more defensive. By teaching students appropriate strategies to use in resolving their differences, you will be assisting them in developing positive problem solving skills.

Distribute a copy of the activity page, *Strategies to Resolve Conflicts*, to each student. Explain to the students that certain kinds of behaviors help people solve their conflicts or problems. Write the following strategies on the board or flipchart. Referring to the activity page, discuss the various strategies for resolving conflicts. These strategies are defined below:

Abandoning: If the people in a conflict situation cannot resolve their differences no matter how hard they try, it may be better to just walk away from the situation.

Apologizing: Saying "I'm sorry" may mean that you are sorry the other person feels the way he or she does; or that both of you contributed to the situation; or that you are sorry the situation happened; or even that you really didn't mean to do whatever you did. It's also a way of reducing the tension and lessening the impact of the situation without necessarily taking the blame.

Avoiding: Sometimes it is just not worth the effort to go along with another person's perception. It is okay to agree to disagree. What you are avoiding is a deeper conflict.

Chance: If you and a friend both want to be first in a game, or one wants to play video games and the other wants to ride bikes, it may be easier to just flip a coin or choose a number between one and ten.

Compromise: Go bike riding first, and then when you are finished go inside and play video games. When you compromise, you give some and take some. Compromising is a win-win situation.

Getting Help: When there is difficulty in resolving differences, it may be beneficial to get help from a parent, teacher, counselor, neighbor, or even an understanding friend. A third perspective is often helpful.

Humor: Making light of a situation may help avoid getting into a deeper conflict.

Postponing: If you are angry or hurt, it may be helpful to put off dealing with the situation until you have calmed down and are able to think more clearly. It also might not be the proper place to express your feelings.

Sharing: There are times when both people realize that they have played a part in the conflict. This is a good time to resolve the conflict by sharing the responsibility of the situation.

After reviewing the strategies with the students, hand out the *Chosen Strategy* activity page. Ask the students to use the *Strategies to Resolve Conflicts* page to choose the correct strategy for each given situation. It would be best for the counselor to go over the situations first, especially with younger students, to make certain they understand the meanings of the strategies and how to use them appropriately. It is also suggested that the counselor walk around the room while the students are working on the activity page to make sure they are doing the exercise correctly, as well as to help anyone who might be in need of added assistance. After the students have completed the activity page, discuss each situation and chosen strategy with them.

Discussion Questions:

1. Which conflict management strategies do you use most often when dealing with your friends?
2. When using the "avoiding" strategy, does it mean that you are staying away from the other person because you are mad at him or her? Explain your answer.
3. In using humor, does it mean that you are laughing at the other person or making fun of him or her?
4. In what kind of situations could you use the strategy of "chance?" In what kind of situations would you not use the strategy of "chance?"
5. Does "apologizing" necessarily mean that you are wrong and the other person is right? Why might apologizing be a helpful strategy even if you feel you didn't do anything wrong?
6. When might "abandoning" as a strategy differ from "giving up?"
7. When you compromise, who wins?
8. What did you learn about using various strategies to resolve conflicts?

Chosen Strategy Answer Key:

1. Abandoning   2. Compromise   3. Getting Help
4. Humor   5. Avoiding   6. Chance
7. Postponing   8. Sharing

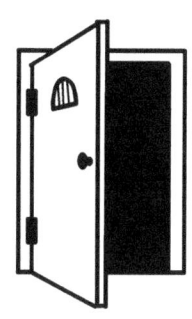

STRATEGIES TO RESOLVE CONFLICTS

ABANDONING
removing yourself from a situation that has no real chance of being resolved

APOLOGIZING
saying "I'm sorry" without necessarily relating that you have said or done anything wrong

AVOIDING
deciding it's not worth the effort and going along with the other person's perception

CHANCE
resolving a conflict by flipping a coin choosing a number between one and ten, or using a similar technique

COMPROMISE
agreeing to give up something to resolve a conflict, with the understanding that the other person will do the same

GETTING HELP
consulting another person (or other persons) to help resolve the conflict when first efforts have failed

HUMOR
lessening anxiety in a conflict by lightening up the situation, while keeping in touch with others' feelings

POSTPONING
agreeing to put off dealing with the conflict until a better time or place

SHARING
when each person takes responsibility for his or her part in the conflict

 # CHOSEN STRATEGY

SITUATION: Maya was upset with Sarah because Sarah kept changing the rules of the game they were playing. She tried to reason with Sarah, but Sarah just wouldn't listen because she wanted to do it her way. No matter how hard Maya tried, she just couldn't seem to get anywhere near resolving their differences. She decided to just walk away and deal with it at another time.

WHAT IS THE CHOSEN STRATEGY IN THIS SITUATION?

_____

SITUATION: Pierre and Carl went to Carl's house after school to play ball, but when they got there, Carl decided that he wanted to go swimming instead because he was hot. The boys started to get into an argument until Pierre came up with an idea that would satisfy both of them.

WHAT IS THE CHOSEN STRATEGY IN THIS SITUATION?

_____

SITUATION: Sandy and Katrina couldn't seem to figure out how to resolve a problem they had involving another friend who was jealous of Sandy and Katrina's friendship. They decided to ask Sandy's mom for advice.

WHAT IS THE CHOSEN STRATEGY IN THIS SITUATION?

_____

SITUATION: Kirnithia saw that her friend, Erin, was getting angry over a silly argument. Kirnithia decided to kid with Erin in a friendly way.

WHAT IS THE CHOSEN STRATEGY IN THIS SITUATION?

_____

 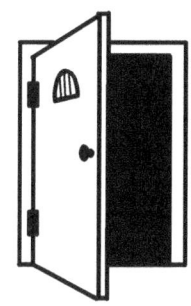

CHOSEN STRATEGY
Page 2

SITUATION: Bart had been having a disagreement with Joshua over which one of them would pitch first in the neighborhood baseball game. Since they were getting nowhere, and Bart really didn't care that much, he decided to give in and let Joshua be the first pitcher.

WHAT IS THE CHOSEN STRATEGY IN THIS SITUATION?

_____

SITUATION: Tara and Susan planned to get together on a Saturday afternoon. Susan wanted to go to the movies, but Tara wanted to go shopping at the mall. They decided to draw straws to see what they would do.

WHAT IS THE CHOSEN STRATEGY IN THIS SITUATION?

_____

SITUATION: Jan's mother was angry because Jan not only came home an hour after curfew, but hadn't finished her homework before leaving the house. Jan's mom decided to take time to "cool off" before deciding on a consequence for Jan's behavior.

WHAT IS THE CHOSEN STRATEGY IN THIS SITUATION?

_____

SITUATION: Ondreka and Charlene have been friends for a long time. Ondreka is quiet and shy while Charlene is outgoing and assertive. The girls got into an argument when Charlene became impatient with Ondreka and called her a "wimp." Ondreka replied with another negative comment. They worked out their conflict by both taking responsibility for their part, recognizing that they had different personalities and needed to respect these differences.

WHAT IS THE CHOSEN STRATEGY IN THIS SITUATION?

_____

ANGRY WORDS

Purpose:

to become aware of various feelings of anger, as well as intensities, that may lead to conflict or harassment

Objective:

Students will learn new words to describe various feelings and degrees of anger.

Materials:

a copy of the activity page, *Angry Words Search*; paper; crayons and/or colored markers; whiteboard or flipchart

Directions:

Anger is a word that everyone knows and has felt at one time or another. Did you know that there are intensities of anger? When two people disagree and don't find a way to resolve their differences, they may become more upset and frustrated. If the disagreement escalates, or gets worse, it may lead to more intense anger as emotions rise. Lying, stealing, put-downs, name-calling, pushing, shoving, threatening, and fighting can lead to various intensities of anger.

Write the following words on separate pieces of paper with a colored marker. (You may choose to use different crayons or colored markers to make the words look more interesting, possibly using orange, red, purple, black, etc. for the anger words with the most intensity).

frustrated, annoyed, irritated, upset, disgusted, uptight, mad, fuming, furious, enraged

Arrange the anger words on the board or flipchart in random order. Discuss the words with the group, beginning with the words that are the least intense and building towards those that are most intense. When all of the words are rearranged from least intense to most intense, review them with the group.

Ask the students which anger word they would probably feel in each of the following situations:

1. Your best friend has a new friend and is ignoring you.
2. Someone stole a book from your desk.
3. A classmate pushed you out of line.
4. Two classmates constantly make fun of the way you dress.
5. A classmate called you "stupid" and the rest of the class laughed.
6. The student sitting next to you keeps putting his elbow on your desk.
7. You feel that the teacher never calls on you to answer a question.
8. One of your friends won't let you sit next to her in the cafeteria; she says she is saving the seat for someone else.

Distribute the *Angry Words Search* activity page to all of the students. Ask the students to circle the "angry words" from the Word List on the activity page. Advise them to look up, down, and diagonally to find the hidden words. Help the students find the first word as an example of how to find and circle the words. You may then choose to either have the students work on the activity (alone or in pairs), or send the *Angry Words Search* home to be worked on with a family member as a follow-up activity.

Discussion Questions:

1. What are some of the new words you learned that mean angry?
2. Which of the anger words on the board or flipchart might be listed under a "Least Intense" list? On a "Most Intense" list?
3. What are some "calming words" that you could use to replace the "angry words" in number two above?
4. Fighting, hitting, punching, yelling, threatening, and name-calling are negative ways to deal with anger. What are some positive ways of dealing with anger?
5. Besides the new words that you have learned that mean "angry," what else have you learned about anger from this lesson?

ANGRY WORDS SEARCH

```
L R T Q J F D S R F D F S E Z
X G F H U B S H R L E U T G Q
B J H M G O X U E D T R O K X
J K I I R I S U I G S I A Q T
K N U C N T T S A D U O D A M
G V A Q R F T P E O G U F U R
Q O D A R U U Y U U S S W K P
Z Q T I R J O R G K I P A I D
M E T B U N S I I N D F Y E D
D H E A N U G P O A Y T T U E
F D L A A N G R Y N T A Q P G
I R R I T A T E D B T E U S A
E S N E T Y D P K I T E D E R
J R J A W E E G G U P X G T N
O W Y Q B R A A I J A L W T E
```

AGITATED   ANGRY   ANNOYED
CROSS   DISGUSTED   DISTURBED
ENRAGED   FRUSTRATED   FUMING
FURIOUS   INFURIATED   IRRITATED
MAD   TENSE   UPSET
UPTIGHT

ANGRY WORDS SEARCH SOLUTION

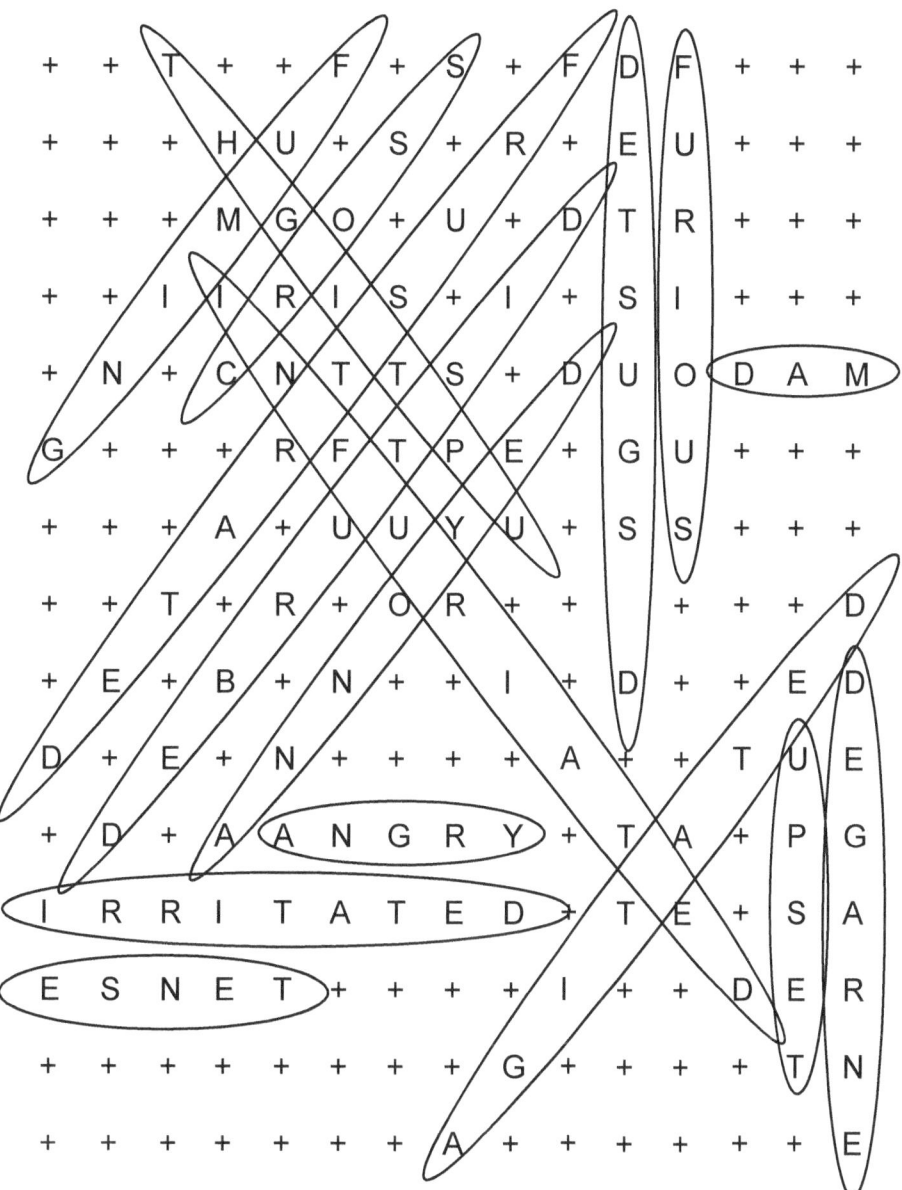

(Over, Down, Direction)

Agitated (8, 15, NE)
Angry (5, 11, E)
Annoyed (4, 11, NE)
Cross (4, 5, NE)
Disgusted (11, 9, N)
Enraged (15, 15, N)
Frustrated (10, 1, SW)
Fuming (6, 1, SW)
Furious (12, 1, S)
Infuriated (4, 4, SE)
Mad (15, 5, W)
Tense (5, 13, W)
Upset (14, 10, S)
Uptight (9, 7, NW)

OUT-STRESSING ANGER

Purpose:

to learn to deal with anger that arises from conflict, pressure, or tension

Objective:

Students will learn various ways of lessening tension and reducing anger.

Materials:

paper, crayons or colored markers, soft music *(optional)*

Directions/Activity:

Conflict, pressure, and tension are normal parts of life. We all have conflicts, even with our family or friends. We all feel daily pressures whether it is related to school, home, or peers. What really matters, though, is not how much pressure or tension we feel, but how we deal with it. It is important that we don't let the tension or anger of conflicts, or the stresses that go along with pressure, get out of control. We need to develop strategies that help us cool off and calm down before we are overwhelmed.

As counselor, or group leader, tell the students about a time when you felt angry or tense, or were involved in a conflict. What positive strategy, or strategies, did you use to deal with the situation? How did you feel before? After?

The following exercises will help your students learn positive ways of reducing the stress or tension involved with conflict or pressure. Choose one or more of the following stress-reducing activities to teach to your students:

Visualizing Your Anger

1. Draw a picture of your anger using crayons or colored markers. Turn the paper over. Imagine your anger disappearing. Now that you are calm, draw a picture of this feeling.
2. Write about your anger: Why are you angry? How do you feel about it? What positive action can you take?

Stress-Reducing Techniques

3. Try each of these stress-reducing exercises:
    a. Tightly clench your fists, and then open them widely. Continue clenching and opening your fists a number of times. Try the same thing with your feet and toes.
    b. Tightly close your eyes and scrunch up your face, then release the tension. Continue this exercise a number of times.
    c. Do ten jumping jacks, or hop up and down on one foot.
    d. Scream without making a sound.
    e. Shake out your whole body.
    f. Take a deep breath in through your nose and hold it for a count of ten. Breathe out slowly through your mouth. Repeat the process a few times.
    g. Close your eyes. Visualize a place that's special to you. Breathe in through your nose and out through your mouth. *(Using soft music is optional.)*

Discussion Questions:

1. Why would expressing your anger in a positive way be best?
2. What might happen if you express your anger in a negative way?
3. What colors did you use in drawing your anger? Why?
4. How would music help in soothing anger? How would visualizing a special place help?
5. How did tensing up and then releasing the tension help reduce feelings of stress?
6. Which activity did you find most helpful for you?

5. Bullying/Harassment

Today, a concern that become even more serious is what we collectively refer to as bullying and harassing behavior. The reach of this behavior has moved beyond the school and classroom to include a virtual sort of behavior now known as cyberbullying. Whatever the source or the setting, there is a real need to work with these issues:

- "I-Messages" are used to help people express how they are feeling about a specific situation.
- Students need to become aware of the different kinds of bullying behaviors, as well as how they can recognize how these behaviors affect others.
- With the advent of the internet, students need to be aware of cyberbullying as a powerful bullying tool, and learn how to deal with it.

COMMUNICATING FEELINGS
"I-Messages"

Purpose:

to communicate to others how you are feeling about an event or situation.

Objective:

Students will gain an understanding of communication by learning to use "I-messages" to express themselves to others.

Materials:

a copy of the *Communicating Feelings* activity page for each student

Directions:

Communication is more than verbal or non-verbal language. We all have our own perceptions and interpretations. Communication takes place only when one person *understands* what the other person means by what he or she is saying.

No one likes to be bullied, threatened, taken advantage of, or embarrassed. "I-Messages" are used to help people express how they are feeling about a specific situation. Often, we send "you-messages" which are threatening and blaming and usually make the situations worse. This activity teaches students the difference between "I-messages" and "you-messages," and the power behind "I-messages."

Begin this activity by giving the students the following example of an "I-message:" *Donald borrowed Matt's skates and left them out in the rain. When he returned the skates, they were rusted. It upset Matt that his skates were ruined.*

Using an "I-message" to express his feelings, Matt might say:

<u>When you</u> borrow my things and ruin them

<u>I feel</u> angry

<u>Because</u> you didn't care enough to take care of them;

<u>What I want</u> is for you to buy me a new pair of skates and to be careful with my things in the future.

With an "I-message," Matt is expressing his feelings without acting out his anger. He is being assertive (making his feelings known) without being aggressive (fighting).

Pass out the *Communicating Feelings* activity page to the students. In a small group or classroom setting, have the students read the various situations and complete the *Communicating Feelings* sentences. Circulate among the students to make sure they understand how to write "I-messages." After the allotted time (approximately 8-10 minutes), ask the students to share one of their answers with the group.

Extension Activity

Have targeted students role-play, or act out, the situations using "I-messages" to communicate feelings.

Discussion Questions:

1. Why is it important to communicate your feelings?
2. Why was this activity helpful in learning to communicate your feelings?
3. What happens when you hide your feelings?
4. Why might others be glad you communicated your feelings?
5. Why might you be glad others communicated their feelings to you?
6. Why is it important in communicating with others that they understand what you mean by what you say?
7. What did you learn through this activity?

COMMUNICATING FEELINGS

1. Mary calls Jimmy "four eyes" because he wears glasses. How can Jimmy communicate how he feels?
   When you _____
   I feel _____
   Because _____
   What I want is _____

2. Julie copied answers from Melanie's test. Melanie had studied hard for the test. How can Melanie communicate how she feels?
   When you _____
   I feel _____
   Because _____
   What I want is _____

3. Lizzy and Maria have been best friends for a long time. Now, Lizzy has a new friend and is ignoring Maria. How can Maria communicate how she feels?
   When you _____
   I feel _____
   Because _____
   What I want is _____

4. Billy constantly bullies David when walking between classes. How can David communicate how he feels?
   When you _____
   I feel _____
   Because _____
   What I want is _____

5. Connie borrowed a book from Juan and didn't return it even after Juan reminded her a few times. How can Juan communicate how he feels?
   When you _____
   I feel _____
   Because _____
   What I want is _____

6. Fran is upset with Asher for passing rumors about her around the class. How can Fran communicate how she feels?
   When you _____
   I feel _____
   Because _____
   What I want is _____

BULLYING BEHAVIORS

Purpose:

to help students recognize different types of bullying behaviors and how to deal with them

Objective:

Students will become more aware of the different types of bullying behaviors, how to recognize these behaviors, and how to deal with them.

Materials:

whiteboard or flipchart

Directions/Activity:

Can someone be a bully without meaning to be? Sometimes it is difficult for a person to recognize the difference between "kidding around" and bullying. What might start off as playful behavior between two or more people can turn into continuing hurtful behaviors that result in bullying. Feelings of stress, pressure, or anxieties can turn into behaviors that are taken out on another person. Sometimes a person becomes a bully because someone else is bullying him or her.

What can a person ask himself or herself to discover if something has become bullying behavior? Some suggestions are listed below:

- *Am I hurting someone's feelings by my "joking" words or actions?*
- *Are my actions hurting someone else physically?*
- *Am I dealing with my anger in an appropriate way?*
- *Do I have the right to try to control someone else?*
- *Would I want to be treated this way?*

Kinds of bullying might include: calling people names, putting them down, or making fun of them. Examples of physical bullying situations would be: knocking into someone on purpose as you go by, tripping another student, or pushing a classmate out of the way at the water fountain.

Discuss the information given above with your students to help them to become aware of the different kinds of bullying behaviors, as well as how they can recognize how these behaviors affect others.

Write the words "bullying" and "harassment" on the board or flipchart. Review the meanings of these two words: (Point out how "torment" is present in both definitions.)

- *Bullying* – teasing, threatening, or tormenting (causing suffering or pain)
- *Harassment* – constant bother, worry, or distress

The following activities can be used in large group or small group settings. Choose one or more of these exercises to use with your students to identify bullying situations and how to deal with them.

1. Have the students use some of the bullying situations given above to develop role-plays. (Remind the students that the emphasis should be on positive methods of dealing with bullying behaviors).
2. Write a list of bullying behaviors on the board or flipchart that are proposed by the students. Then, discuss different suggestions for handling these situations.
3. Assist the students in making a book about bullying behaviors and how to deal with them. Students may work individually, in pairs, or in small groups to illustrate handling different situations.
4. Have the students form dyads. Ask them to interview each other about a time that they were bullied or harassed by someone else. Tell them to use made-up names, not real ones, when relating the situation. Afterwards, allow some of the students to relate their partner's story to the whole group.
5. Write a letter to a make-believe bully, letting him or her know what is being done, how you feel about it, and what you would like the bully to do to change his or her behavior.

Discussion Questions:

1. How would you define bullying? Harassment?
2. Do you think someone could show bullying behaviors without meaning to?
3. Can you always tell the difference between when a person is bullying or just kidding around? What is the difference between the two?
4. What are some non-physical bullying behaviors that involve feelings?
5. What are some bullying behaviors that are physical?
6. If a person uses "control" to bully other people, what can those people do to take this control away from the bully without giving back the same bullying behaviors in return?
7. What are some ways to handle bullying that you learned from participating in the activities above?
8. What has this lesson taught you about your own behaviors?

CYBERBULLYING:
A Powerful Bullying Tool

Purpose:

to raise awareness in students of cyberbullying and its destructive impact on children and adolescents

Objective:

Students will become more aware of the definition of cyberbullying and will gain a better understanding of the impact that it has on others

Materials:

whiteboard or dry-eraser board; five (5) sheets of newsprint, one for each small group

Directions:

According to Webster's Dictionary, a bully is "a blustering, browbeating person; especially one who is habitually cruel to others." Bullying is a form of open, aggressive behavior that is intentional, hurtful, and repeated. It includes embarrassment, unkind teasing, malicious rumors and gossip, threats, and exclusion. People who bully generally want to have power over others. Although a number of children who bully have low self-esteem, others may have high self-esteem and feel they are better than others. Whatever the reason, bullying hurts for a long time, and can cause children to not want to go to school or become lonely, sad, or depressed.

Bullying takes place in the classroom, cafeteria, and on the playground; on the school bus; and more recently, through technology. This powerful bullying tool, known as cyberbullying, includes: use of e-mails, instant messaging (IMs), blogs, chat rooms, or social Web sites; text or photo messages; and/or phone calls to intentionally and repeatedly harass, threaten, or ridicule others.

Begin this activity by writing the following types of cyberbullying on the board:

- e-mails/instant messaging (IM)
- blogs, chat rooms, or social Web sites
- text messages
- photo messages
- phone calls

Divide the students into five (5) groups. Review the five different types of cyberbullying that are on the board. Then, give the following example of cyberbullying: *Joseph pulled his cell phone out of his book bag and snapped a picture of Madelyn, a chubby classmate, as she jokingly pushed a large piece of cake into her mouth. That night, he forwarded the picture to everyone on his contact list with the message: "Oink, oink! Piggy piggy!" The next day, a number of students called out, "Oink, oink! Piggy piggy!" much to Madelyn's embarrassment. Others joined in thinking it was funny. Still others just looked on or turned away without a word. This harassment continued for quite a long time.*

Discuss this example with the group as a whole. Explain the differences among the bully, the victim, and the bystander (one who stands by and does nothing). *Who was the initial bully?* (Joseph; the others who followed Joseph were also adding to the bullying behavior); *the victim?* (Madelyn); *the bystander(s)?* Any student who watched or heard and did nothing to try to stop the bullying behaviors. *This scenario is just one example of cyberbullying.*

Assign each small group a type of cyberbullying from the list on the board, saying: *Write a scenario about your type of cyberbullying. Then, either illustrate the scenario or make it into a skit. After 15 minutes, each group will present their activity to the whole group.* (Papers may be taped to the board.)

Discussion Questions

1. What did you learn from this activity?
2. What is meant by the following statements: Bullying helps no one – and hurts everyone.? Is the behavior hurtful or helpful?
3. How can bullying cause harm way beyond hurtful feelings?
4. Why has cyberbullying become such a "hot topic?"
5. What do you think the term "bullycide" is referring to? *(Bullycide is a new word that has been coined because of the number victims of bullying ending their own lives.)*
6. If the victim or another person tells an adult about the bullying behavior, is that person considered a tattletale? *(Tattling means trying to get someone in trouble; telling means trying to stop trouble.)*
7. What has this lesson taught you about your own behaviors?

6. DIVERSITY/TOLERANCE

Today, more than ever, diversity and tolerance play a crucial role within our communities and throughout the world. Schools are among the first institutions to absorb the cultural fluctuations brought about by immigration and other factors. The activities in this section focus on the following issues:

- It is important for people to accept others without being judgmental, and to take responsibility for their own words and actions.
- At a very early stage, children develop awareness of and prejudices against people who are different.
- By becoming more familiar with physical, communicative, and learning disabilities, students can better understand people who have them.

STAND UP AND BE COUNTED

Purpose:

to gain an understanding of tolerance and good character

Objective:

Students will learn that what they say and do is important, and that it takes courage to be able to say "no, that is not acceptable."

Materials:

a copy of the activity page, *Tolerance and Good Character Statements*, for each student; one piece of colored construction paper for each student; crayons and/or colored markers; scissors; stapler

Directions:

Discuss with the students that *tolerance* has to do with respecting the beliefs, cultural differences, customs, and rights of others. It is not acceptable to make fun of, threaten, or bully someone else. It is important for people to accept others without being judgmental, and to take responsibility for their own words and actions. Remind the students of the Golden Rule: to treat others as you would want them to treat you.

Discuss how "good character" involves respecting others, showing responsibility, displaying loyalty, caring about others, being thoughtful, and standing up for what is right.

Tell the students that they will be doing an activity that will help them better understand tolerance and good character. Allow each student to choose a piece of colored construction paper and a crayon or colored marker. Each student will also need a pair of scissors, or you may choose to have them shared.

Have the students take off one shoe and trace that foot on the piece of construction paper. Then have them cut out the traced foot. Ask the students to write their names on the bottoms of their foot cutouts.

Hand out the *Tolerance and Good Character* activity page to the students and discuss the written statements with them. Ask the students if they have any ideas to add to the lists. Discuss their ideas and have them write them on the activity page under "added statements."

Following a discussion of the activity page, ask the students to choose one of the statements that has special meaning to them and neatly write that statement on their own foot cutout.

Call on students who want to share with the class. Have these students read their statements to the other students and explain why they chose these statements (why the statements were important to them).

Collect the foot cutouts, staple them together, and form a chain across (or around) the room. Count the number of students in the class or group. Count the number of foot cutouts that are stapled together. Emphasize how *everyone* needs to "stand up and be counted."

Discussion Questions:

1. What do you think it means to "stand up and be counted"?
2. What is meant by tolerance?
3. What are some examples of "good character"?
4. Why does it sometimes take courage to say: "no, that is not acceptable" to a group of schoolmates?
5. What does bullying mean? Does it only mean to hurt or threaten someone physically?
6. How can words hurt?
7. What does it mean: "A chain is only as strong as its weakest link?" How would that pertain to a classroom or a group? Can you give any examples?
8. How would it be if everyone lived up to the ideals of tolerance and good character? What role does each person play?

TOLERANCE AND GOOD CHARACTER STATEMENTS

Statements:

I will not accept language that hurts.
I will not laugh when someone makes fun of someone else.
I will not make fun of anyone.
I will not put someone down with words or body language.
I will not call people names.
I will not intimidate or threaten someone else.
I will not try to embarrass someone else.
I will not bully others.
I will not stand by and let someone else hurt others.

I have a responsibility to make others feel safe and accepted.
I will think twice before I say something or do something that may be hurtful.
I will take responsibility for my own words and actions.
I will strive to be thought of as a person who stands up for what is right.
I will accept people for who they are without being judgmental.
I will treat people with the same respect that I would want from them.
I will value friendships and not put conditions on them.

Added statements:

UNDERSTANDING TOLERANCE

Purpose:

to help students understand the meanings of words that are often used to describe and promote the concept of tolerance

Objective:

Students will be able to understand and use words that define the issue of tolerance.

Note to Counselors: This lesson may take from one to three sessions to complete, depending upon the age of the students and time allotment.

Materials:

a copy of the activity page, *Defining Words That Deal With Tolerance*, for each student; a copy of the activity page, *Defining Words Match-Up*, for each student; board or flipchart

Note to Counselors: These activity pages are best used, as written, with students in grades 5 – 8. Counselors may choose to select some of the words from the word list that would be appropriate for use with younger children. The *Defining Words Match-Up* activity page can be modified using only those words that were selected from the word list.

Directions:

At a very early stage, children develop awareness of and prejudices against people who are different. Family, peer groups, language, and institutions reinforce stereotypes and prejudices that are prevalent in our society. The words that children are exposed to either reinforce prejudice or instill beliefs of tolerance and acceptance of the value of diversity. Children often criticize the differences they see in others because they don't understand or value these differences.

Students may hear words that support and encourage *tolerance*, but often times have difficulty defining these words. The following activity will give students the opportunity to gain an understanding of these words and be able to utilize them in discussions concerning tolerance. The Discussion Questions provide an opportunity to expand the students' understanding of the value of tolerance.

Give each student a copy of the *Defining Words That Deal With Tolerance* activity page. Begin the lesson by telling the students the following: *We live in a world that is uniquely diverse. What that means is that people are the same in some ways and different in others. It is easier to get along with those people we feel are most like us. We recognize similar features, and better understand common backgrounds and ways of life. It is important, however, to also learn to appreciate the differences among people. In order to learn to value the differences, as well as the similarities of people, we need to gain an understanding of their cultures, customs, and beliefs.*

Today we are going to be discussing words that have to do with the issue of "tolerance," which means respecting the beliefs and practices of others. We hear these words all around us: within our families, neighborhoods, and communities, and on radio and television. Learning the meanings of these words will not only allow you to use them, but will help you become more aware of your attitudes and ways of thinking.

Using the *Defining Words that Deal with Tolerance* activity page as a reference, discuss the definitions of the words that are listed. After going over the definition of a word, you may want to give it more meaning, for example, you might say:

> ***Attitude*** *is defined as a "way of thinking, feeling, or acting." What is your attitude about school? Do you think of it as an opportunity to learn or do you think of it as something you have to do? What is your attitude about girls playing football? Do you think it is only a boy's sport or do your think that anyone who wants to can play? What is your attitude about people from other countries? Do you think they are "different," or do you believe that everyone has similarities and differences, and that is okay? What is your attitude? How do you think, feel, and act?*

Since a number of the words in the list are very much alike in definition, you may want to group the words according to the similarities among the words, for instance:

- ethnic, race, culture, and multicultural
- attitude, prejudice, discrimination, stereotype, and racism
- fairness, respect, consideration, thoughtfulness, and
- tolerance
- caring, love, empathy, understanding

There are a number of alternatives for introducing these words to the students:

1. Write the groups of words on the board or flipchart. Discuss the definitions of the words as they appear in the various groups.

2. Discuss the words as they appear on the activity page. Following the discussion, have the students work <u>individually</u> to group the words according to the similarities among the words.

3. Discuss the words as they appear on the activity page. Following the discussion, have the students work in <u>pairs</u> as they group the words according to the similarities among the words.

After discussing the definitions of the words, have the students turn their activity page over and put it aside. Next, hand out a copy of the *Defining Words Match-Up* activity page to each student. Instruct the students as follows: *We have just learned the definitions of a number of new words. They are not easy words to define, but they are important words. By understanding the meanings of these words, you will understand more about the issue of "tolerance."*

You have just been given an activity page for matching the words we have (just) discussed with their definitions. (You may want to assign this activity page on the following day if you find yourself short of time; if so, review the words with the students before assigning the activity page). *Many of the words are similar, but they all have to do with the same issue of "tolerance." The words are listed at the top of the page with their definitions listed below, A through R. Let's do the first definition together. Definition "A" says: " just, honest, and equal for everyone." Now find the word at the top of the page that matches this definition.* Call on a student to give the answer, which is "fairness." Then, tell the students to put the letter "A" on the space provided next to the word, "fairness."

Give the students this "hint:" *If a word is a correct answer, it will not appear in the definition. For example: If the definition is, "showing concern or consideration for others," the correct answer cannot be "consideration" because it appears in the definition. It works the same way for the following definition, "knowing, respecting, and being tolerant or sympathetic toward others." The correct answer could not be "respect" or "tolerant" because they appear in the definition.* Ask the students if they have any questions before they begin. If you need to give one more explanation of the "hint," use the following example: *The definition, "manner that shows courtesy, consideration, or high opinion" has the word "consideration" in it. Therefore, "consideration" could not be the correct answer, because it is used in the definition.*

Instruct the students to begin the activity page. Move around the room while the students work to see how they are doing and to offer help if needed, especially with the younger children.

When the students have completed the activity page, have them get out their list of words and definitions *(Defining Words That Deal With Tolerance)*. They may work individually, or in pairs, to check their answers on the *Defining Words Match-Up* activity page. After about 8-10 minutes, or earlier if they finish quicker, review the answers with the whole group.

Defining Words Match-Up Answer Key:

_H_	Tolerance	_B_ Attitude	_J_ Prejudice
_C_	Discrimination	_I_ Stereotype	_R_ Culture
_D_	Ethnic	_N_ Race	_E_ Racism
_K_	Multicultural	_A_ Fairness	_M_ Respect
_L_	Caring	_O_ Thoughtfulness	_F_ Consideration
_Q_	Empathy	_P_ Understanding	G Love

Discussion Questions:

1. What is meant by: *We live in a world that is uniquely diverse*?
2. Can you give an example of how a friend could be the same in some ways, and yet different in other ways?
3. Why do you think it is easier to get along with people we feel are most like us?
4. Why is it important to learn to appreciate the differences among people?
5. If you were trying to explain the meaning of tolerance to another person, what would you tell him/her?
6. What do the following groups of words have to do with tolerance: (You may want to put the words on the board or flipchart).
   - *ethnic, race, culture, multicultural*
   - *attitude, prejudice, discrimination, stereotype, racism*
   - *fairness, respect, consideration, thoughtfulness, tolerance*
   - *caring, love, empathy, understanding*
7. In what way has this lesson been most meaningful to you?
8. How do you feel you will benefit in the future from what you have learned through this lesson?

DEFINING WORDS THAT DEAL WITH TOLERANCE

Tolerance – allowing other people to have opinions or follow customs that are different from one's own; respect for the beliefs and practices of others

Attitude – way of thinking, feeling, or acting

Prejudice – a negative judgment or opinion formed before knowing the facts; dislike or hatred of a particular group, race, or religion

Discrimination – distinctions or differentiations made on the basis of preference or negative opinions

Stereotype – an overly simple picture or opinion of a person, group, or thing

Culture – the behavior patterns, arts, customs, beliefs of human work and thought

Ethnic – relating to large groups of people sharing a common racial, national, religious, linguistic (language), or cultural heritage

Race – a human population distinguished by inherited physical traits or characteristics

Racism – the belief that a particular race is superior to or better than another; discrimination or prejudice based on race

Multicultural – of or including more than one culture or ethnic group

Fairness – just, honest, and equal for everyone

Respect – manner that shows courtesy, consideration, or high opinion

Caring – being concerned or interested

Thoughtfulness – showing concern or consideration for others

Consideration – thoughtfulness or kindness towards others

Empathy – experiencing the feelings, thoughts, or attitudes of another person, or seeing the world through his or her eyes

Understanding – knowing, respecting, and being tolerant or sympathetic toward others

Love – the ability to care for others

DEFINING WORDS MATCH-UP

Words

_____ Tolerance   _____ Attitude   _____ Prejudice
_____ Discrimination   _____ Stereotype   _____ Culture
_____ Ethnic   _____ Race   _____ Racism
_____ Multicultural   _____ Fairness   _____ Respect
_____ Caring   _____ Thoughtfulness   _____ Consideration
_____ Empathy   _____ Understanding   _____ Love

Definitions

A. just, honest, and equal for everyone
B. way of thinking, feeling, or acting
C. distinctions or differentiations made on the basis of preference or negative opinions
D. relating to large groups of people sharing a common racial, national, religious, linguistic (language), or cultural heritage
E. the belief that a particular race is superior to or better than another; discrimination or prejudice based on race
F. thoughtfulness or kindness towards others
G. the ability to care for others
H. allowing other people to have opinions or follow customs that are different from one's own; respect for the beliefs and practices of others
I. an overly simple picture or opinion of a person, group, or thing
J. a negative judgment or opinion formed before knowing the facts; dislikeor hatred of a particular group, race, or religion
K. of or including more than one culture or ethnic group
L. being concerned or interested
M. manner that shows courtesy, consideration, or high opinion
N. a human population distinguished by inherited physical traits or characteristics
O. showing concern or consideration for others
P. knowing, respecting, and being tolerant or sympathetic toward others
Q. experiencing the feelings, thoughts, or attitudes of another person, orseeing the world through his or her eyes
R. the behavior patterns, arts, customs, beliefs of human work and thought

GETTING ACQUAINTED WITH DIVERSITY
Physical, Communicative, and Learning Differences

Purpose:

to make students more aware of physical, communicative, and learning differences (or disabilities) and more understanding of people who have them

Objective:

Students will be able to recognize the similarities and differences between themselves and people who have physical (visual impairment), communicative (hearing impairment), and learning differences (or disabilities).

Materials:

Physical Differences: a copy of the activity page, *Paper Blindfold*, for each student, scissors, roll of tape; a few objects that make sounds, i.e.: bell, whistle, two sticks, harmonica or recorder, etc. (counselor's choice); a few objects that feel different to the touch, i.e.: smooth, fuzzy, rough, sharp (counselor's choice)

Communicative Differences: a copy of the activity page, *Everyday Sounds*, for each student

Learning Differences: mirror, pencil, a half-sheet of unlined paper for each student, a piece of cardboard or file folder

Directions:

The terminology, "physical, communicative, and learning differences," is used in this lesson, rather than the more familiar term, "handicaps." The word "disability," which is also used, does not refer to a lack of ability. Instead, the ability to see, hear, or learn is accomplished in a variety of ways. It is important for students to understand that people who have disabilities can achieve many of the same things they do. People with disabilities just accomplish these things in different ways.

The various disabilities that are targeted in this lesson – visual impairment (difficulty seeing, or blindness), hearing impairment (difficulty hearing, or deafness), and learning impairments (or disorders) – will be dealt with separately. **Since related activities will be presented with each disability, it will take more than one session to cover all of these areas.**

Introduce this lesson to the students as follows: *There are both similarities and differences among people. Everyone has feelings about how they look, what they can do, and what they cannot do. Some things are the same; some things are different. Something that is easy for one person may be difficult for another person. One person may be good at math, or sports, or singing. Another person may find math complicated, but find reading easy.*

We are going to become more familiar with physical, communicative, and learning disabilities so that we can better understand people who have them.

Physical Differences: Visual Impairment

*Let's begin our lesson this morning (afternoon) by learning, in a small way, what it feels like to have a physical difference called **visual impairment**. This disability can be caused by heredity, by disease, or by injury to the eye(s). People who have difficulty seeing well wear glasses in order to see more clearly. When people can't see at all, they have to learn new ways to deal with this disability, called "blindness."*

People who cannot see often have to rely on other senses such as hearing and touch. The activity you are about to take part in will help you visualize how these senses are used to help blind people "see."

Hand out a copy of the *Paper Blindfold* activity page to each student. Ask the students to cut the paper into three strips by cutting along the dotted lines. Then, have the students tape the three strips together, forming one long strip that will be used as a blindfold. Tape the paper blindfolds over each student's eyes.

Next, give the following instructions: *We are going to allow your minds to get a "glimpse" of what you hear. I will make a sound. When you hear it, raise your hand. I will call on a student and ask what he or she hears. After a student answers correctly, I will go on to another sound. Let's see how your hearing helps you to "see" what I am doing. Here is the first sound. Listen closely and raise your hand when you think you know what it is:* (Below are some examples the counselor can use)

- Blow a whistle.
- Ring a bell.
- Tap two sticks together, or clap your hands.
- Knock on a door, or open and close the door.
- March across the room.
- Move a chair from one spot to another.

After you have completed a number of sounds, give the students the next instructions: *Do not remove your blindfolds. I am going to move around the room with an object in each of my hands. I will give everyone an opportunity to feel the objects.* Walk around the room with two different objects in each hand, i.e., smooth, fuzzy, rough, and sharp. After every student has had the chance to touch the objects, put the objects out of sight and continue with your directions: *You may now take off your blindfolds. Raise your hands if you can describe one of the objects you touched. What did it feel like? What do you think it was? Give a number of students an opportunity to describe the objects. Then ask the following Discussion Questions.*

Discussion Questions: (Visual Impairment)

1. How did you feel once the blindfold was put over your eyes?
2. How did your sense of hearing help you to visualize what you were hearing?
3. How did your sense of touch help you visualize what you were feeling?
4. Did you find that you had to concentrate on your senses of hearing and touch more than when you can see without the blindfold?
5. Did this demonstration help you to become more aware of what it might feel like to be visually impaired?
6. What might be the similarities and differences between a sighted person and a visually impaired person? (Emphasize that there are other differences than just the sight, i.e., *likes and dislikes, cultures, physical characteristics, etc.*)

Communicative Differences: Hearing Impairment

This lesson will help to make you more aware of what it is like to have a communicative difference called **hearing impairment.** *People who are hard of hearing, or have difficulty hearing, can sometimes wear a hearing aid to help them hear better by magnifying the sounds, or making them louder. If a person cannot hear at all, he or she is said to be deaf. People who are deaf can communicate in a different way from people who can hear. By using finger spelling and sign language, people who cannot hear can spell and speak with their fingers and hands.*

We are going to do an activity that shows another way for people who cannot hear to communicate with both people who can hear, and people who are deaf. This way of communicating is called lip reading. People who are hard of hearing learn to read lips much like they learn to read. It takes studying and practice.

I am going to stand in front of the room and say something to you. If you think you can read my lips, raise your hand and I will call on you. We will do this exercise slowly since you haven't learned this method of communication.

Below are some sentences to use as examples with the students. **Mouth the words slowly and distinctly.** The sentences should become more difficult as you continue, but not too difficult for the students to comprehend.

Start by saying: *the first sentence is:* "My name is_____ . Repeat the sentence a second time. Give the students a chance to respond. Then, continue with the other sentences, one at a time. The following sentences are examples. You may make up some or all of your own.

- *What is your name?*
- *The boy is very tall.*
- *Bobby likes to play football.*
- *Mary likes to read books.*

After presenting these simple sentences, try some of the following ones that give directions. Tell the students to respond to what you are saying by carrying out the action:

- *Put your hands over your ears.*
- *Scratch your head.*
- *Shake your head "no."*
- *Stand up; turn around; and sit down.*

Now, give a copy of the activity page, *Everyday Sounds*, to each student. Introduce this exercise by saying to the students: *There are sounds all around us. Sometimes we aren't even aware of them because we aren't concentrating. Perhaps there are some sounds that we haven't heard because of where we live or what we have or haven't experienced. The activity page in front of you has a list of sounds that appear in everyday life. Read each sound and check "yes" if you have heard it before, and "no" if you haven't. Are there any questions?* If not, the students may begin. When you have finished, go over the following Discussion Questions.

Discussion Questions: (Hearing Impairment)

1. What did you have to do in order to be able to read lips? On what did you have to concentrate? Did you find it easy or difficult? Why?

2. Did this demonstration help you to become more aware of what it might be like to be hearing impaired?

3. What might be the similarities and differences between a person who can hear and a person who is hearing impaired? *(Emphasize that there are other differences than just the hearing, i.e., likes and dislikes, cultures, physical characteristics, etc.)*

4. What do you think it might feel like not to be able to hear these sounds? How do you think you might be able to communicate these sounds without hearing them? (For example, a person who cannot hear the sounds can still see the action of what is happening).

5. Do you think that people who can hear take sound for granted? Why?

6. As you go through your day today and through the night, try to be more aware of the sounds around you. See if you recognize sounds that you weren't aware were there. Do you think you will need to concentrate on the sounds or listen to them more closely?

EVERYDAY SOUNDS

HAVE YOU EVER HEARD THE SOUND OF:	YES	NO
THE POP OF A BALLOON?		
OCEAN WAVES?		
CHILDREN LAUGHING?		
A PLANE FLYING IN THE SKY?		
CLAPS OF THUNDER?		
HAIL FALLING ON THE ROOF?		
THE WIND IN THE TREES?		
A CAR DRIVING BY?		
A SCHOOL BELL RINGING?		
A BABY CRYING?		
A PERSON YAWNING?		
A BAT HITTING A BASEBALL?		
A CAT'S MEOW?		
A WASHING MACHINE?		
WATER BOILING ON THE STOVE?		
A DOORBELL RINGING?		
POPCORN POPPING?		

Learning Differences: Learning Disabilities

Note to the Counselors: Learning disabilities, or disorders, can be divided into a number of categories. Some of these include:

- Disorders of motor activity involve hyperactivity (always moving, impulsive); hypoactivity (quiet and lethargic); incoordination (physical awkwardness, clumsiness).
- Perceptual disorders (difficulty organizing and interpreting information, i.e., reversing letters and numbers).
- Attention disorders (unable to focus and then break attention when appropriate).

Students with learning disabilities may be placed in a regular classroom but meet with a resource teacher for individualized instruction at certain times during the day. Inclusion is a newer concept whereby students with learning disabilities are placed in a regular classroom with a general education teacher and a learning disabilities teacher working together in the classroom as a team.

The following activity helps students who do not have learning disabilities develop an understanding of students who do have one or more types of learning disabilities.

Instruct the students as follows: *Some people with learning differences perceive, or recognize, things differently. Their brains have difficulty organizing and understanding images and information. Letters and numbers may look backwards or reversed. Sometimes this is known as mirror images. The activity that you are about to do will help you understand how confusing this type of learning disability can be.* (Be sure to emphasize that having a learning disability does not have anything to do with intelligence. A person can be gifted in intelligence and still have a learning disability.)

Attach a mirror to the wall behind a desk. Select students to come to the desk one at a time and to place a piece of writing paper on the desk. Hold or position a piece of cardboard, or a file folder, in such a way that the students who come up to the desk will not be able to see their hands but will be able to see the image of their hands in the mirror. Tell the students the following: *Look at the mirror, not at your hands. Write your name at the top of the paper. Write a sentence complimenting a friend.* As the students finish their turns, have them return to their seats. When all of the students have had an opportunity to participate in the mirror image activity, go over the following Discussion Questions with them.

Discussion Questions: (Learning Disabilities)

1. What happened with your hands when you were writing while looking into the mirror?
2. How did it feel while you were doing this activity? Did it feel awkward? Frustrating? Stressful?
3. Did you feel successful? How do you think a person feels who doesn't feel successful?
4. How do you think a person with this type of perceptual disorder feels when they try to write?
5. Does having a learning disability have anything to do with a person's level of intelligence? *(Emphasize again with the students that a learning disability has nothing to do with a person's level of intelligence. It is the way the brain perceives objects and images.)*

 # PAPER BLINDFOLD

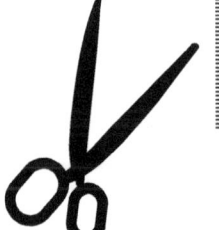 

7. GOALS/ORGANIZATION

In order to be successful in life, students need to define future goals and plan toward achieving them. The activities in this section focus on the following issues:

- Being better-organized and using time wisely will help students reach their goals.
- Successful people maintain a positive attitude, a sense of responsibility, and an awareness of the value of teamwork.
- In preparing for the future, it is the earnest effort that students put forth that help them reach their goals.

USING TIME WISELY

Purpose:

to develop a sense of using time wisely in pursuit of goals

Objective:

Students will gain a clearer perspective on how to become better organized toward reaching their goals in school.

Materials:

whiteboard or flipchart

Directions/Activity:

Students may know the goals they wish to reach in school, but don't always know how to go about accomplishing those goals. Being better-organized and using time wisely will help students reach their goals. The following large group (classroom), counselor-directed activity, *Using Time Wisely*, will help students gain a clearer understanding of wise uses of time and unwise uses of time. Before the students begin the activity, tell them to consider how they can use time more **wisely**.

Discuss with them some of the ways they can use their time in a more productive way:

- When getting ready for school
- During the school day?
- With their homework
- At home
- At play

Remind the students to also consider how time is used unwisely at school, at home, and at play.

Direct the activity, *Using Time Wisely*, in the following manner:

1. Have each student make two lists: *Wise Use of Time* and *Unwise Use of Time*.
2. Put the students in pairs. Have them compare their lists, putting the lists together to form two new lists. They must come to an

agreement of wise and unwise uses of time in forming the two new lists.

3. Put two pairs of students together forming groups of four students to a group. Again, have the students compare their lists. Coming to an agreement, have them put their lists together to form two new lists: wise and unwise uses of time.

4. Have each group of four choose a representative to read his or her group's lists to the class. Work together, as a class (or large group), to form two final lists on the board or flipchart: *Wise Use of Time* and *Unwise Use of Time*.

5. Go over the Discussion Questions with the students.

Discussion Questions:

1. What did you learn from this activity?
2. How does it help you to separate wise uses of time from unwise uses of time?
3. What have you discovered that you have been doing that would go on the *Wise Use of Time* list? The *Unwise Use of Time* list?
4. Do you use time more wisely at school, at home, or at play?
5. What changes in your use of time will help you be more organized and assist you in reaching your goals?
6. Why is it foolish to waste your time?
7. Why was it beneficial to work alone, next in pairs, then in foursomes?

S.M.A.R.T.
Success Measures Attitude, Responsibility, and Teamwork

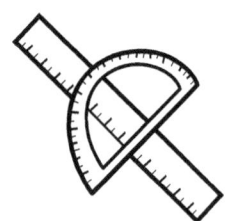

Purpose:

to gain insight into the meaning of success as it relates to attitude, responsibility, and teamwork.

Objective:

Students will gain a better understanding of how a positive attitude, sense of responsibility, and ability to work together as a team leads to success in school and in life.

Materials:

a copy of the activity page, *Thinking S.M.A.R.T.,* for each student; whiteboard or flipchart

Directions:

Generally, people think that being successful in school means making A's, or being successful in life means having a lot of money, new cars, and a big, expensive house. Often times, success is equated with ownership and power. But, what does it really mean to be successful? This lesson emphasizes the importance of attitude, responsibility, and teamwork in becoming a successful person. A positive attitude leads toward making the best of every day and each situation. It facilitates perseverance in striving to reach goals. Successful people maintain a sense of responsibility. They take control of their words and their actions, and accept the consequences of their behaviors. We know that people do not live in a vacuum. To be successful, they need to develop the values of teamwork: giving and taking equally, listening actively, sharing ideas, compromising, and working together as a team to reach their goals.

To introduce this lesson, write "**S.M.A.R.T.**" on the board or flipchart. Go over the meanings of the letters: "**S**uccess **M**easures **A**ttitude, **R**esponsibility, and **T**eamwork." Then, discuss the following with the students: *What does it mean to be successful? Does it mean making a lot of money or having a big house? Does it mean having a new shiny car or fancy computer system and big screen T.V.? How do we truly measure "success?"*

Success is measured by the **attitude** *you have. Do you look on the bright side of life and try to make the best of each day? Do you keep trying to reach a goal without giving up when it gets difficult? Do you treat other people the way that you want to be treated?*

*Success is measured by your sense of **responsibility**. Do you take responsibility for your behaviors – for what you say and what you do? Can you say "no" to others when it is in your best interest? Do you follow through with tasks to the best of your ability? Do you blame others when things don't go the way you expect them to, or do you take responsibility for what has occurred and make necessary changes?*

*Success is also measured by **teamwork**. Do you work well with others in a group situation? If you take the role of leader, do you "guide" or do you "boss?" If you take the role of team member, do you work hand-in-hand with the other team members to accomplish your goals? Do you offer your ideas, yet listen to others, as well? What do you do to draw silent members into the group activities? Do you share, compromise, and resolve issues or concerns before they get out of hand? What part do you play in teamwork to help your group be successful?*

Give out a copy of the *Thinking S.M.A.R.T.* activity page to each student. Discuss with the students how they feel they have measured, or shown, a positive attitude, responsibility, and teamwork in school and/or at home. Instruct the students to answer the true/false questions on the activity page by circling the T or F in front of each question. Ask the students to explain their answers in the spaces provided below the questions. Work the first true/false question with them as an example. After the students begin their work, walk around the room and give assistance if necessary.

Thinking S.M.A.R.T. Answer Key: T, T, F, F, F, T, T

Discussion Questions:

1. What does S.M.A.R.T. (Success Measures Attitude, Responsibility, and Teamwork) mean to you?
2. Can you think of a time that you changed a negative attitude to a positive attitude and it made a difference in your behavior and the consequences of that behavior?
3. Give an example of a time that acting responsibly made a difference at school or at home.
4. What have you experienced working as a team member of a group at school that was negative? Positive?
5. Would the word "Trying" be considered a measure of success if it were substituted for the word "Teamwork" in the title?
6. How would you personally define or measure "success"?
7. What is one way that you are on the path to success?

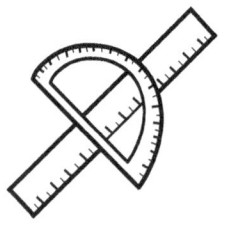
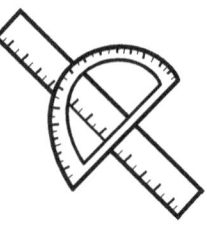

THINKING S.M.A.R.T.
Success Measures Attitude, Responsibility, and Teamwork

T F Having the right attitude makes it easier to make smart life choices.
Explain: _____
_____

T F What you do each day in school prepares you for the future.
Explain: _____
_____

T F If you are an "A" student, your classmates will think you're a nerd, and you won't have as many friends.
Explain: _____
_____

T F It is your teacher's responsibility to make sure you do your class work, and your parent's responsibility to make sure you do your homework.
Explain: _____
_____

T F If you are working on a group project, it doesn't matter who does the work in the group as long as it gets done.
Explain: _____
_____

T F Negative thinking can lead to a negative attitude that, in turn, can lead to negative behaviors and consequences.
Explain: _____
_____

T F Organization and preparation in your work will lead toward success both in school and outside of school.
Explain: _____
_____

EARNEST EFFORT

Purpose:

to help students recognize that earnest, or serious, effort is the key to reaching their goals, both in and out of school

Objective:

Students will gain an awareness of the need to put forth earnest, or serious, effort in order to fulfill their goals, prepare for the future, and succeed in life.

Materials:

a copy of the activity page, *Earnest Effort*, for each student; a copy of the activity page, *Interview Form: Earnest Effort*, for each student; whiteboard or flipchart

Directions:

What does it take to succeed in life? In what ways might you prepare for the future? What interesting questions to pose to your students. Some of the answers might be:
- Setting short-term and long-term goals
- Being organized
- Using time wisely
- Showing responsibility
- Completing tasks
- Having pride in your work

All of the above factors are important in preparing for the future and succeeding in life, but the "glue" that puts it all together is the constant, serious *effort* that a person puts forth in reaching his or her goals. This earnest effort is shown through diligence, or by careful or continued work. The following activity, *Earnest Effort*, helps students realize the part that effort plays in accomplishing their objectives. This lesson will be presented in two parts: Part I is an activity that will be done in class. Part II will be completed at home and reviewed in class.

Part I: Hand out a copy of the activity page, *Earnest Effort*, to each student. Write the word, "earnest" on the board or flipchart. Instruct the students as follows: *In front of you, you have an activity page called, "Earnest Effort." "Earnest" may be a new word for you. What do you think it means?* Call on a few students to answer (or guess). *The word "earnest" means serious. So we* *are talking about serious effort that is put forth by each person to do the best that he or she can do.* Write "diligently" on the board or flipchart. *Putting forth effort means working "diligently;" that's another new word for you! It also means to put forth effort by working carefully and continuously.*

The activity you are about to do concerning diligence, or effort, has two parts. Part I will be done in class. Part II is an interview to complete at home and bring back to school. We will discuss Part II together in a follow-up lesson. Go over the various exercises on the *Earnest Effort* activity page with the students. Tell them that they will choose one of the three activities listed under Part I to answer.

Give the students 10-15 minutes to complete the activity of their choice in Part I. After the allotted time, review the Discussion Questions for Part I with them.

Part II: This activity is for the students to complete at home. Hand out the activity page, *Interview Form: Earnest Effort*, to each student. Explain the assignment as follows: *You are being asked to use this "Interview Form" with a parent, relative, or neighbor in discovering how diligence, or earnest effort, has played a part in his or her life. The questions are listed for you on the interview form with spaces underneath them for the answers.* Ask the students to bring their interview assignment back to school the next day, or on a day of your choosing. (The Discussion Questions for Part II will be discussed after the students return with their completed assignment).

Extension Activity:

Have the students who chose #3 on the *Earnest Effort* activity page get together to act out the role-play in front of the whole group.

Discussion Questions: (Part I)

1. What does the word earnest mean?
2. How might putting forth earnest effort be the "glue" that helps a person reaching his or her goals?
3. For those of you who chose #1 on the activity page: How did diligence, or effort, help you in your work at school? How did it help you with improving your work and work habits?
4. For those of you who chose #2 on the activity page: What are some ways that practicing diligence, or earnest effort, has helped you at school and at home.
5. For those of you who chose #3 on the activity page: What did you learn from your role-play situation?

Discussion Questions: (Part II)

1. Whom did you interview concerning how diligence, or earnest effort, has played a part in someone's life? What did you learn from your interview?

2. Is there anything that you learned that might make a difference in the way you prepare for your future?

3. What did you learn in the interview that helps you visualize, or picture, what it takes to succeed in life?

 # EARNEST EFFORT

Part I: (Choose one of the following.)

1. Write about a situation where diligence, or earnest effort, helped you in your work in school. In what ways did careful and continuous effort in various subjects help you in improving your work and work habits?

   _____
   _____
   _____
   _____
   _____

2. List 6-8 ways that practicing diligence, or earnest effort, has helped you at school. List 6-8 ways that practicing diligence, or earnest effort, has helped you at home.

   _____
   _____
   _____
   _____
   _____
   _____
   _____
   _____

3. Create a role-play for two or three people concerning the following situation:

   Your friends want you to go outside to play softball. They insist that they need you on the team because you are a good player. You have homework to do before you go to a Tai Kwon Do lesson at 6:30 p.m. It is now 4:00 p.m. and you haven't started your homework yet. What would you do?

INTERVIEW FORM
EARNEST EFFORT

Student's name _____ Date _____

Who is the person being interviewed:
  parent ____ relative ____ neighbor? ____ other? _____

If parent: Mom? ____ Dad? ____ Stepmom? ____ Stepdad? ____
If relative: What relation is this person to you? _____

Interview Questions:

1. How has diligence, or earnest effort, played a part in your life?

2. How has constant hard work helped you get where you are today in your job or career?

3. How has constant hard work helped you get where you are today in other areas of your life?

4. How did the effort you put forth in school help you in achieving your goals?

5. What advice would you give me concerning the importance of the diligence, or earnest effort, I put forth in my own life?

8. TRANSITION/MOBILITY

Significant changes and problems can develop for children because of such events as relocation, immigration, and grade/school advancement. The activities in this section focus on the following issues:

- Once students share interests, hobbies, and likes and dislikes with each other, they become more open to forming friendships within their new surroundings.
- Students need to understand the changes that will occur and the challenges they will face as they move from elementary school to junior/middle school, and then on to high school.
- Students who are new to the country or the community need to become more aware of feelings they may experience, such as isolation and loneliness.

WORKING WITH IMMIGRANT FAMILIES
Information for Counselors

*The U.S. Bureau of the Census indicates that as many as
one out of every 10 children in the United States is foreign born.
According to New York City Board of Education statistics,
the New York schools enrolled students from more than 140 countries who spoke
178 different languages and/or dialects.*

Schools are among the first institutions to absorb the cultural fluctuations brought about by immigration. The cultural shock often felt by immigrant students as they enter an unfamiliar realm produces feelings of heightened confusion and isolation. Unless there is the support of an understanding and welcoming staff and student body, the process of acculturation can be frightening and disturbing to the immigrant student.

Often times, immigrant students prove surprisingly resilient and eager to mimic the behaviors and values of their American peers. Parents, however, generally find it more difficult to adapt to the new culture. Conflicts may develop between children intent on change and parents determined to preserve traditional values. They also may have difficulties helping their children with their homework if the language and educational system is foreign to them.

Immigrant families face many challenges. Although their histories may differ, some factors are commonly shared:

- The greater the cultural and language differences are, the more difficult is the adjustment.
- Migration due to political violence, war, or other trauma may leave room for little choice or planning.
- The length of time a family has been in the U.S. is a determinant of the amount of stress involved.
- Depending on socioeconomic status, immigrants often struggle with employment, income, and housing.
- Immigrants often leave behind family, friends, and other people they relied upon for support.

As a counselor, you must not only be sensitive to and have knowledge of your own cultural and personal values, but to similarities and differences between yourself and immigrant families within your school. Some of the cultural factors that need to be addressed include:

- Understanding your own culture in order to better understand others.
- Being aware of differences in communication styles and patterns, including body language.
- Checking with the other person during communication to see if your interpretation is correct
- Knowing about a student's culture not only by reading, but also through observation, asking questions, and exploring differences, as well as making adjustments to your communication style.

Specific areas of information that would be beneficial in working with immigrant families includes:

- Learning about the family history.
- Knowing how many people speak English in the home.
- Understanding what a typical day and weekends are like.
- Finding out about their school expectations, and noting the roles that teachers, parents, and administrators played in their homeland's educational system, as well as determining if there are any major concerns.
- Relating information about the community and its resources.
- Discovering any areas of expertise, i.e., abilities, talents, hobbies, or work (both here and in their homeland).

Counselors can gather information concerning various cultures through ESOL teachers, the school system's multicultural department, and/or community agencies that work with immigrant families. A resource that I have used, and would highly recommend to others for a more in-depth understanding of what counselors can do to facilitate their working with immigrant students and their families, is listed below:

Reaching Out To Immigrant Parents: What Educators Can Do by Cristina Casanova, Innerchoice Publishing, (877) 799-5350

COOPERATIVE GROUP PICTURE

Purpose:

to help classmates get to know each other in a new school or new classroom setting

Objective:

Students will become better acquainted with members of their small group, as well as the class as a whole, by working together in a cooperative, cohesive manner.

Materials:

construction paper, crayons and/or colored markers, whiteboard or flipchart

Directions:

Imagine being a new student in a new school. As you walk into the classroom, you look around the room. There is not a familiar face anywhere. You feel totally alone and, possibly, like you don't have a friend in the world. There are many questions racing through your mind, your stomach is in knots, and you just know that everyone is looking at you.

Transition is unique for each child, but all new students have a need to belong. Some of the issues facing new students include gaining peer acceptance, gaining acceptance from their teacher(s), understanding expectations (both behaviorally and academically), and adjusting to the new school environment. These students may have come from another city or state. If they have moved from another country, there may be issues of cultural differences, traumatic stress, separation, deprivation, and/or isolation. Besides adjusting at school, many of these students are adjusting to a new home and neighborhood, while their parents may be adjusting, as well. There are other home issues that may be prevalent in the family's move to a new neighborhood, or new city or state, i.e., divorce or separation, a change in a parent's job/business, military assignments, seasonal work for migrants, or economic difficulties. Whatever the reason for the move, the student often faces changes at home, as well as at school.

Whether students are entering a new school, or a new classroom at the beginning of the school year, there is a certain amount of apprehension and anxiety in meeting their new classmates.

This activity will help the students get to know each other in a comfortable, non-threatening atmosphere. Once students share interests, hobbies, and likes and dislikes with each other, they become more open to forming friendships within their new surroundings.

Tell the students that they will be working in small groups to create a Cooperative Group Picture. Write the terms "composite" (picture), "cooperation," and "cohesiveness" on the board or flipchart. Discuss the terms with the students.

> *Composite:* a whole made up of different parts
> *Cooperation:* working together toward a common end
> *Cohesiveness:* sticking together as a group

Divide the large group (or class) into small groups of four or five students. In their small group settings, the students will offer information about themselves as to their special traits (including physical characteristics), likes, and/or interests, (i.e., I like to read; I like to play piano; I like to shop for clothes; I like to play soccer; I like to do math, etc). After each person has a turn describing himself or herself, the group members will produce a cooperative group picture, drawing one composite person that represents all of their group members. Have all of the group members sign their composite picture.

When the students are finished with their drawings, each group will select one person to be the spokesperson for that group. Each small group spokesperson will then describe his or her group's picture with the large group, or class as a whole.

Discussion Questions:

1. How well did you know your small group before beginning the activity? After?

2. How did it make you feel doing this activity?

3. What other special traits, likes, and/or interests do you have that weren't shown in the picture?

4. Could you use all of your special traits, likes, and/or interests in the group picture? Why not? Was it difficult choosing which ones you would use?

5. Did you feel there was a sense of cooperation and/or cohesiveness among your group members? Why or why not?

6. What did you learn from this activity?

TRANSITION TO JUNIOR/MIDDLE AND HIGH SCHOOLS

Purpose

to help students prepare for the transition to junior/middle and high schools, and become acquainted with the changes that take place during these points in time, both personally and socially

Objective:

Students will become more prepared for the transition to junior/middle and high schools, and more aware of the changes that occur during these time periods, both personally and socially.

Materials:

a copy of the activity page, *Character Values From A to Z*, for each student; a classroom dictionary for each student

Directions:

The first transition for the elementary age student is the move to junior/middle school, followed by the changeover to high school just a few years later. Some of the changes that take place may include:

- A larger school building that feels like a maze of classrooms and special areas, along with a feeling of the need for roller skates to make it from class to class on time.
- New class schedules, along with a variety of new teachers who have different teaching styles.
- Becoming accustomed to where they are supposed to be and when they are supposed to be there.
- Building new friendships; a number of schools feed into the new school, bringing with them a whole group of fresh faces.
- No longer being the "big shot" in the school; students are now "low man on the totem pole."
- New rules and academic challenges, including organization, note-taking skills, and more homework.
- Added peer pressure stemming from a stronger need to belong, and/or be a part of a group.
- Physical, social, and emotional changes.

This lesson will help students develop an awareness of these changes and become acquainted with a better understanding of the challenges they face. To introduce this lesson review the above information with the students.

The questions listed below may be used to stimulate discussion.

1. How do you feel about going to junior/middle school (or high school) in a new, larger building? What are the concerns you might have?

2. Do you feel confused right now about new kinds of schedules, and/or getting to classes on time?

3. What is your feeling about having a number of new teachers with differing (different) teaching styles and expectations?

    What are "teaching styles?" *Explain that "teaching styles" are approaches, manners, or techniques of teaching. Each teacher has his or her own style.* What is meant by "expectations?" *Explain that "expectations" have to do with what the teacher expects of you as far as homework, conduct, and effort.*

4. How do you feel about meeting new students in the school you will be going to? Have you even thought about it? Do you feel comfortable, or do you feel anxious or nervous?

5. Are you excited about the prospect of making new friends, or are you apprehensive or worried about fitting in?

6. If you are changing classes and teachers for each subject and special area class (i.e., Physical Education, Foreign Language, Elective, etc.), how do you picture yourself handling the change?

7. How do you feel about any possible peer pressure in your new environment? Do you feel strong enough to be able to choose positive influences rather than negative ones? Do you think you will be able to make wise choices, even if you are pressured?

8. What physical, social, and/or emotional changes do you think will probably occur over the next few years? *Bring out that the students will grow and mature physically, become more influenced by peers, and develop new interests and concerns. Their changes may also impact their relationships with their friends.*

Following your review and discussion of the above information, hand out the activity page, *Character Values from A to Z*, to each student. Begin the exercise by saying: *How you react to the challenges of the transition to junior/middle school (or high school) is very much related to your character values and your self-esteem (how you feel about yourself). Some of the positive character values that you might choose to describe yourself might be: nice, thoughtful, studious, vivacious (lively or cheerful), or serious. There are many character values that you can choose to portray yourself. The activity page you have in front of you gives you the opportunity to think about the qualities you possess: how you see yourself, and how others might possibly see you. This activity page is filled with letters of the alphabet. Your assignment is to choose a different character value that begins with a letter of the alphabet, from A to Z, as it describes you. The first one, A, gives you a positive quality choice to circle, or you may add one of your own in the space provided. You may use a dictionary to help you if you get stuck on any of the letters.* After answering any questions the students may have, instruct them to begin. Allow 15-20 minutes to complete the activity page. Then ask the students to put a star next to the five character values that they feel are most important to them, and/or that best describe their positive qualities.

Discussion Questions

1. How did it feel to think about the character values you possess? Did you realize that you had so many positive qualities?
2. If your classmates filled in the activity page with your qualities, do you think it would look the same as yours? Why, or why not?
3. What are the five character values, that you starred on your paper, that you feel are most important to you, or best describe you?
4. What did you discover about yourself through this activity?

Extension Activity:

Materials:

a copy of the activity page, *Turning the Negative into the Positive*, for each student

Directions:

Give each student a copy of the activity page, *Turning the Negative into the Positive*. In the spaces provided on the activity page, have the students list any negative personal qualities that they feel they may have. Next to the negative qualities, have them write what the opposite positive qualities would be. Then, ask them to write how could they go about achieving the positive qualities. An example might be:

Negative Quality: quick temper   *Positive Quality*: staying calm

How I would go about achieving the change:

I would try to take deep breaths and count to ten before responding; I would "think and act" instead of "react."

Allow time for the students to complete their activity page, then review their responses with them. Encourage the students to make an effort to develop the positive qualities they have identified.

Discussion Questions: Extension Activity

1. What are some negative qualities that you recognize in yourself?
2. How could you turn those negative qualities into positive values? What might you do?
3. What gain is there in changing negative qualities into positive ones?
4. What did you discover about yourself through this activity?

CHARACTER VALUES FROM A TO Z

A able animated adventurous

B _____

C _____

D _____

E _____

F _____

G _____

H _____

I _____

J _____

K _____

L _____

M _____

N _____

O _____

P _____

Q _____

R _____

S _____

T _____

U _____

V _____

W _____

X _____

Y _____

Z _____

TURNING THE NEGATIVE INTO THE POSITIVE

Negative Quality _____ Positive Quality _____
   How I would go about achieving the change: _____
   _____
   _____

Negative Quality _____ Positive Quality _____
   How I would go about achieving the change: _____
   _____
   _____

Negative Quality _____ Positive Quality _____
   How I would go about achieving the change: _____
   _____
   _____

Negative Quality _____ Positive Quality _____
   How I would go about achieving the change: _____
   _____
   _____

Negative Quality _____ Positive Quality _____
   How I would go about achieving the change: _____
   _____
   _____

Negative Quality _____ Positive Quality _____
   How I would go about achieving the change: _____
   _____
   _____

CIRCLE OF FRIENDS
Outside / Inside

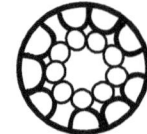

Purpose:

to help students gain an understanding of what a person might feel like when he or she is new to a school, as well as help students become more aware of the feelings that the new student experiences

Objective:

Students will be become more aware of feelings, such as isolation, loneliness, and sadness, that a new student might feel when trying to "fit in" with their new peers as a part of the group or class.

Materials:

whiteboard or flipchart

Directions/Activity:

They come to the counseling office, one by one, a cloud of gloom looming over them. They sit in the big chair in my office, slouching over, eyes diverted toward the ground. As they raise their head in answer to my greeting, I tune in to the looks of sadness, confusion, and loneliness that are transparent on their faces and in their body language. These are the students, over the years, who are new to our school. They may have come from another country, state, city, or town; or, they may have moved to our school from another facility not too far away.

Wherever these students have come from, they all have one thing in common. They have moved away from school sites with which they were familiar, leaving behind friends, teachers, and other supportive people, venturing into a new learning environment. These are the new students who are looking to "fit in," as they long for acceptance and inclusion among their new peers.

This lesson will benefit not only students who are new to the school, but also those students who may feel excluded from their peer groups for other personal or social reasons. All students will become more aware of feelings such as isolation and loneliness, through participating in the following activity.

Begin the session with the students by saying: *There are a number of students each year who come to our school from another country, state, city, or town. Maybe some of them have come from another nearby school. Wherever they come from, they have one thing in common. They want to feel accepted by their classmates. This is not much different from a student who has been at our school for a long time, but has difficulty making friends or being included with groups of their peers.*

You are going to take part in an activity called, "Outside/Inside" that will help you gain a better understanding of what it feels like to be excluded from a group of your peers, or classmates. You will experience the difference between tight-knit or closed groups that shut others out, and open groups that not only welcome others, but also allow them to move freely from group to group.

This lesson can be in a large group or small group setting. If it is in a large group setting, form small groups around the room of approximately 6-8 students. In a small group setting, you will have only one group. The following instructions will be geared toward a small group setting.

Choose a student from the group who is a more assertive, self-assured child to act as the "new student who is trying to become a part of the group." Then, have the rest of the students form a closed, tight-knit circle by putting their arms around the waists or shoulders of the persons who are at their sides. Give the following instructions to the students: *The circle you have formed represents a group of peers, or classmates, who are friends. They work and play together at school, and even at times outside of school. They do not allow others to become part of their group.*

Write the expression, "tight-knit, on the board or flipchart. Then explain the terminology: *The word "tight-knit" is a way of describing an item of clothing, like a sweater, that is so tightly knitted, that nothing can get in between the stitches. You are formed into a tight-knit circle without spaces between you. The "new student," is going to try to become a part of your group. She (or he) wants to be accepted and included as a new friend. As part of the circle of friends, you will not allow the "new student" to enter this tight-knit circle. She (or he) will go around the circle, attempting to find a space to enter. She (or he) will not be able to find this space. Are there any questions?*

Have the students begin the exercise. Give them a full minute to allow the "new student" an opportunity to find a space to get through the circle of friends. After you give the signal to stop, give the following directions: *Now, I'd like you to step back and form a larger circle. Hold hands, allowing a space between you and the persons who are at your sides. The same "new student" will try to become a part of your group. This time, you will permit her (or him) to not only enter the group, but also allow her (or him) to freely go in and out.* (If it is a large group setting, the "new students" from each group may go in and out of each other's group.)

After a full minute, have the students stop the exercise and return to their seats. Ask the "new student" to stand up. (If it is a large group, all of the "new students" will stand up). Go over the following Discussion Questions with first the "new student (s)," and then the whole group (or class). (The "new student(s)" may sit down after the first part of the discussion).

Discussion Questions:

"New Student(s)"

1. How did it feel to be the "new student?"

2. How did it feel to be excluded from the group during the first part of the activity? Did you feel isolated or left out? Were you sad, anxious, or confused?

3. What happened when you were permitted to enter the circle during your second attempt? Did you feel more included? Did you feel more accepted by your peers? How did you feel being a part of the group?

Whole Group (Or Class)

4. How did it feel to be one of the accepted members of the circle of friends, or group?

5. What happened when the "new student" tried to become a part of the tight-knit group? How did you feel? Did you find yourself not willing to move to let her (or him) in? Is this the way you might actually be if a new student wanted to become a part of the circle of friends?

6. Did you feel differently when the "new student" was permitted to enter the circle of friends and become a part of the group? Can you explain this feeling?

7. Which group do you think the "new student" felt he or she fit-in with the best ... the first tight-knit group, or the second open group?

8. This lesson is called "CIRCLE OF FRIENDS: Outside / Inside". Why do you think this is an appropriate title for the activity you just experienced?

9. Why is it important to welcome new students and make them feel that they are a valued member of your group or class?

10. What are some of the things that you can do to make a new student feel welcome?

9. CHILDREN OF DIVORCE

With an increase in occurrence of divorce and/or separation, more and more children are faced with subsequent feelings and emotions. The activities in this section focus on the following issues:

- Children of divorce need to learn to cope with altered lifestyles, as well as any new feelings or behaviors that may arise.
- In order for children to be able to discuss their emotions, they must be able to define them in terms of how they feel.
- Children's feelings may be suppressed due to fear, embarrassment, sadness, or loneliness; or may be acted out as a result of anger, frustration, confusion, or resentment.

IT'S NOT YOUR FAULT
Children of Divorce

Purpose:

to help students deal with divorce (or separation) issues

Objective:

Students will better understand how to deal with the issues and feelings of divorce (or separation).

Materials:

a copy of the activity page, *It's Not Your Fault*, for each student

Directions:

Children's reactions to divorce (or separation) and periods of adjustment are varied. Although they may respond to divorce differently, there are some general characteristic reactions. Children may think they are responsible for their parents' divorce or think their behavior has been a contributing factor. There also may be feelings of guilt for not having prevented the separation. Children have feelings of anger, fear, confusion, and/or frustration that are being suppressed. Feelings of sadness, embarrassment, shame, loneliness, and/or helplessness may also be underlying concerns.

Divorce often results in a change in living conditions. Children may need to learn to cope with altered lifestyles, as well as any new behaviors that may arise. To be able to deal with issues and feelings of divorce, children must be given an opportunity to express their thoughts and feelings in a safe environment. They also need to understand that whatever feelings they may experience are normal.

It is best to have a small group setting of 4-6 students when helping children cope with issues of divorce (or separation). The following activity will help students have a better understanding of their feelings and behaviors. Although this activity is designed to use with small groups, it is also appropriate to use with individuals who may not be ready for a group setting.

1. In a small group setting, have students form a circle. Discuss the various issues, concerns, and/or feelings that are described above. Be sure that all of the students have a chance to express their

feelings. Bring out the observation that students may share many of the feelings that they have heard expressed during the group discussion.

2. Following the initial discussion, give each student a copy of the *It's Not Your Fault* activity page. Review the questions with the students before asking them to complete the activity page. You may want to go over one question at a time, giving the students time to write their answers on the activity page before going on to the next question. There may be a need to use more than one group session for this activity.

3. When the activity page is completed, have the students put their names on the back of their papers, and then collect the papers. After reviewing the papers, you may want to have a follow-up session with the group to discuss pertinent issues or concerns. You may find that one or more of the students may benefit from individual counseling, as well.

Discussion Questions:

1. What did you learn from this session?
2. Do other students share any of the feelings you have or had?
3. How might the things you learned during this session help you cope with your parents' divorce (or separation)?
4. How might you help a friend who is in the same situation?
5. Do you feel differently now (after this activity) than you did before? If so, in what way?

 # IT'S NOT YOUR FAULT

1. Children often feel that their parents' divorce or separation is their fault, that they somehow are to blame. Do you feel that you did something to make the divorce happen? Explain your answer.

2. It is normal to feel sad, angry, confused, or worried. How do you feel about your parents' divorce or separation? Why do you think you feel that way?

3. If parents do not still love each other, it does not mean they do not love you. How do you feel about this statement?

4. Some things change during and after a divorce or separation. What things do you feel have changed in your life (either at school, at home, or both)?

5. Have you noticed a change in school concerning your concentration, your attitude, and/or grades? If so, have you talked to your teacher about it?

IT'S NOT YOUR FAULT
Page 2

6. What do you feel are the negative changes in your life?

7. Do you feel there are any positive changes in your life?

8. Do you feel you are pulled in different directions since your parents aren't living together? (For example, perhaps you have to carry messages back and forth between parents, or want to spend more time with one of your parents).

9. If you live in two different houses or apartments, how do you go about organizing your time and your belongings (clothes, toys/games, school books, etc.)?

10. Often times, it is hard to talk to your parents (or one of your parents) about how you are feeling. Is there anything special you would like to be able to tell your parents (or one of your parents)?

PUZZLING EMOTIONS
Divorce and Separation

Purpose:

to gain an understanding of emotions involved with situations of divorce and separation

Objective:

Students will be able to use feeling words in describing emotions associated with family divorce and separation.

Materials:

a copy of the activity page, *Puzzling Emotions*, for each student

Directions:

There are all kinds of confusing emotions experienced when children are involved in their family's divorce or separation. In order to be able to discuss these emotions, they must be able to define them in terms of how they feel. The *Puzzling Emotions* activity page is a non-threatening way of helping children deal with their issues concerning divorce and separation. They also discover that everyone has feelings and emotions.

In a small group setting of 4-6 or 6-8 students (depending on the ages), discuss the following feeling words with the students:

*anger   fear   confusion   frustration   sadness   shame
embarrassment   loneliness   helplessness   safety*

Ask the students what they think each word means. Then ask them if they have ever felt that way. As counselor, or group leader, you may add to the definitions or give examples to help clarify the meanings.

Following the discussion, have the students complete the *Puzzling Emotions* activity page. The students may work alone or in pairs. When everyone has completed the puzzle, go over the answers with the group members.

Puzzling Emotions Answer Key:

*Across: 3. helplessness 5. confusion 6. safety 8. fear 9. sadness
Down: 1. embarrassment 2. loneliness 4. anger 6. shame 7. frustration*

Discussion Questions:

1. What are two things you learned from this session?
2. Why might you feel shame or embarrassment because of your parents' divorce or separation?
3. Why do you think you might feel a sense of loneliness even if you have a lot of friends?
4. In what ways might you feel a sense of helplessness due to your parents' divorce or separation?
5. Even if you feel sad because of your parents' divorce or separation, is it okay to feel happy at times because of other situations in your life? Do you feel guilty when you feel happy?
6. Why do you think there are so many feelings of confusion and frustration?
7. What might cause a sense of fear when parents' get divorced or separated?
8. Why is your sense of safety threatened when your parents' get divorced or separated?
9. How has it helped you to discuss issues dealing with divorce or separation?

PUZZLING EMOTIONS

Across:
3. defenseless or without power
5. misunderstanding or mix-up
6. protection, security, or well-being
8. fright or alarm
9. unhappiness, sorrow, or grief

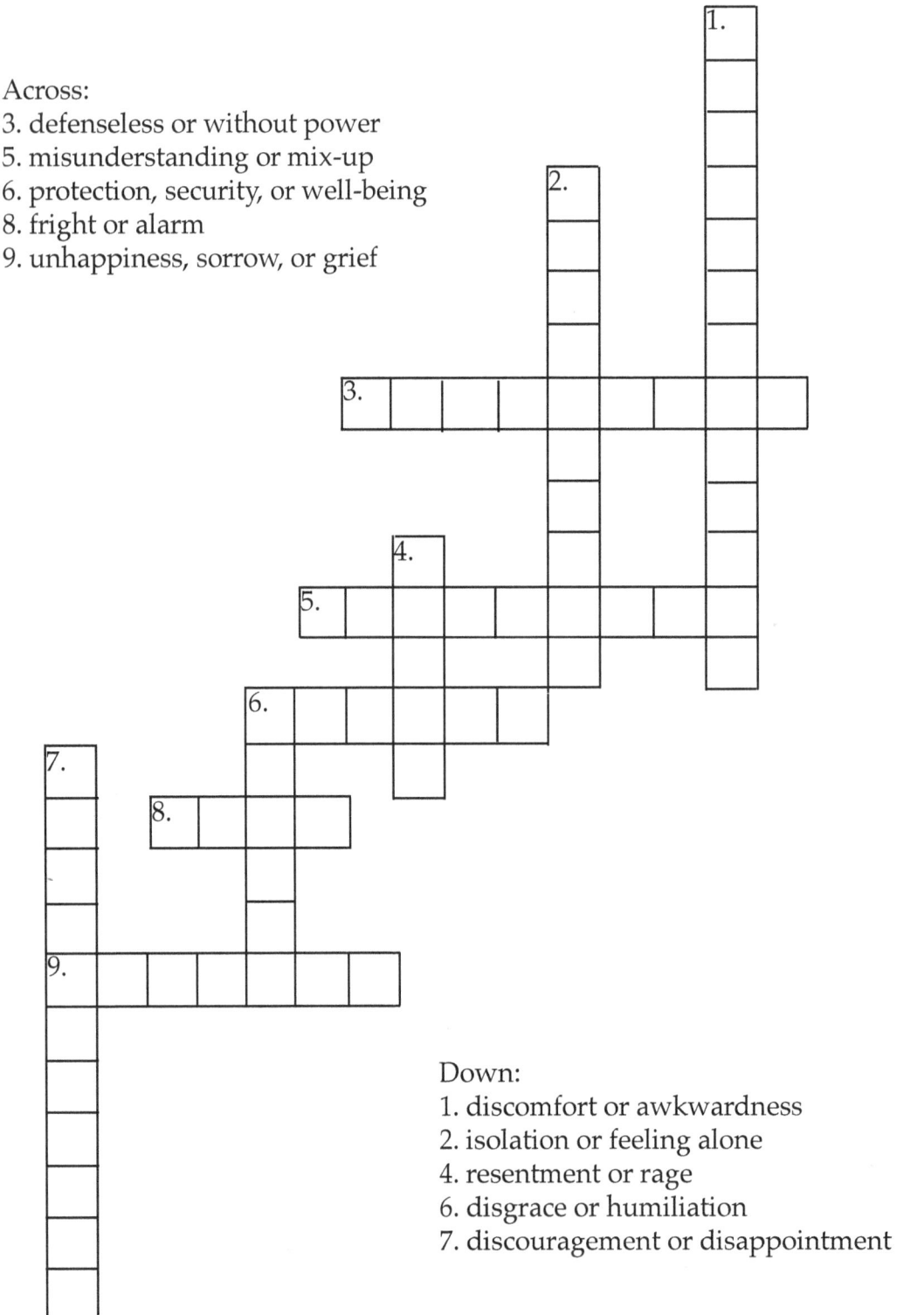

Down:
1. discomfort or awkwardness
2. isolation or feeling alone
4. resentment or rage
6. disgrace or humiliation
7. discouragement or disappointment

WHAT I THINK – WHAT I FEEL

Purpose:

to provide children of divorce (or separation) a safe environment where feelings may be expressed, explored, and clarified

Objective:

Students will be able to gain a better understanding of their thoughts and feelings as they learn to cope with the circumstances of their parents' divorce (or separation).

Materials:

a copy of the activity page, *What I Think – What I Feel (Sentence Completion)*, for each student

Directions:

The inability to express thoughts and feelings is a problem experienced by children of divorced (or separated) parents.

Feelings may be suppressed due to fear, embarrassment, loneliness, or sadness. Anger, frustration, confusion, or resentment may be acted out with inappropriate behaviors. Children (or adolescents) may be afraid or ashamed for their friends to learn that their parents are no longer living together. The protected environment of a small group setting allows the students to face these fears and negative thoughts. Feeling safe within the small group may also allow students to be able to open up with their parents and relatives. It is important to remind students about confidentiality – *what we say in the group, stays in the group.*

The following *I Think – I Feel* activity page is designed as a sentence completion exercise to enable students to start exploring their thoughts and emotions. The counselor will hand out an activity page to each student instructing the students as follows: *Let's explore some of the thoughts and feelings you carry around throughout each day. What are these emotions and how do you deal with them? What are some of the changes you have been through or are still going through? How did you feel when you first found out about your parents' divorce? How do you feel about your friends knowing? What are some of the negative aspects of the divorce? Are there any positive effects of the divorce? Answer the sentence completion exercise that has just been passed out to you. Sometimes, writing the first thing that comes into your head expresses your real thoughts and feelings. After all of you have finished, you may choose to share some of these feelings with the rest of the group. You do not have to share if you don't want to.* (Students who choose not to share at the beginning of discussion, may enter in later.)

Collect the activity pages from the students at the end of the session. Put each student's name on the back of his or her paper. After reviewing the papers, keep them in a file. You may find areas that need further discussion in the group setting. You may also decide that one or more students might possibly benefit from individual counseling to deal with specific issues or concerns.

Extension Activity:

Students in the intermediate grades may gain insight into what they think and how they feel from role-playing, or "counseling" each other, with reference to the situations on the *I Think – I Feel* activity page.

Discussion Questions:

1. How did it feel to answer the questions concerning divorce?
2. Why do you think it might have been upsetting to you?
3. Did it feel comforting in any way to be able to express your feelings?
4. Were there any questions that you hadn't thought about before?
5. Before this activity, did you think you were the only one who felt the way you do? What did you think after the activity?
6. What did you learn from this lesson that will help you cope with the divorce situation?
7. What did you learn from this lesson that you can share with your parents?

 # WHAT I THINK – WHAT I FEEL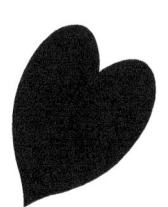

Sentence Completion

1. When my parents first told me they were getting divorced, I felt _____
_____

2. The way I feel about divorce is _____
_____

3. I need to talk to my parents about _____
_____

4. Something that worries me is _____
_____

5. When I first told my friend(s) about the divorce, I thought _____
_____

6. The person I can best talk to about the divorce is because _____
_____

7. Negative (bad) things about the divorce are _____
_____

8. Some positive changes that I see because of the divorce are _____
_____

9. One of the things I miss most is _____
_____

10. Something I could say to help a friend whose parents are getting a divorce is _____
_____

11. When I am upset with one of my parents, I _____
_____

12. If I could change one thing about my attitude or behavior now, I would _____
_____
_____

PARENT PERMISSION LETTER
Children of Divorce

Because of the sensitivity of issues of separation and divorce, it is advisable to send a parent permission letter home to be signed by the parent/guardian. The following **sample** letter may be used or modified to meet your needs.

Dear Parents,

The counseling program at our school offers individual counseling, classroom guidance, parent-teacher conferences, and small group sessions that deal with specific concerns. Topics such as making friends, peer relationships, communication skills, decision-making skills, conflict resolution, and handling peer pressure are offered.

Your child has been invited to join one of the groups that deals with communicating in the family. Many students feel that the concerns they are having are unique. In the group, they discover that there are others who have the same problems they do. For students who have been through a divorce or separation, it is often a comfort to learn how to adjust to the situation and communicate better with family members.

Your son/daughter, _____ has expressed an interest in being a part of this group. Please sign and return this letter with your child. If you have any questions or concerns, please call me at (phone number).

Sincerely,

(Name)
Counselor

_____   _____
Parent Signature   *Date*

10. GRIEF AND LOSS

Children are especially vulnerable in dealing with loss. They often lack the understanding and/or coping skills needed to get through the grieving process. The activities in this section focus on the following issues:

- All people have feelings. What is different is the way they react to these feelings.
- The need to communicate feelings of loss is vital in order to help the child move through the stages of grief.
- As children go through the time of sadness, or grieving, they may be holding on to thoughts that they need to be able to express.

EXPRESSING FEELINGS OF GRIEF AND LOSS

Purpose:
to deal with sadness, anger, confusion and other feelings of grief and loss

Objective:
Students will be able to express their feelings in dealing with grief and loss, as well as better understand that all people experience the same feelings, but in different ways.

Materials:
a copy of the activity page, *Expressing My Feelings of Sadness*, for each student; whiteboard or flipchart

Directions/Activity

Part I: There are no good or bad feelings. There are just feelings. Some feelings feel better than others. We *all* have feelings. In that way, we are all the same. What is different is the way that we react to these feelings. In any given situation, each person will react in his or her own way.

The following activities will help students to understand feelings and learn to express them. This lesson may take two or three sessions to complete, depending on the ages of the students, and their needs to move a little more slowly in discussing their feelings.

In a small group setting of 6 - 8 students (depending on the age level), tell the students that they will have an opportunity to discuss a number of feelings that they experience. Write the following words on the board or flipchart and briefly discuss them with the students:

Angry, Shocked, Sad, Guilty, Lonely, Confused,
Helpless, Uneasy, Scared, Depressed, Overwhelmed

Have the students form dyads, or pairs. After the dyads are formed, the students will decide who will speak first and who will speak second. They will then choose a feeling word from the above list. The first speaker will tell about a time he or she felt that way, i.e., angry, shocked, sad, etc. *(whatever word was chosen).* After about 1-2 minutes, depending on the age of the students, ask them to switch roles so that the second speaker can talk about the same feeling word.

At the end of the first round, have the student who spoke first stay seated and have the person who spoke second move to a new partner. The person who moved becomes speaker #1 and the new partner becomes speaker #2.

Repeat the process a few times depending on the allotted time for the lesson, leaving about 10 minutes for a follow-up discussion.

Have the students return to their original seats for a whole group discussion. Choose 2 or 3 students to share one of the feeling words that they discussed in their dyads. This should take only a couple of minutes. Afterwards, go over the discussion questions with the whole group.

Discussion Questions: Part I

1. How did it feel discussing these feelings with your partners?
2. In what ways were your feelings the same? Different?
3. Do you think it was easier to share your feelings with one person rather than the whole group? Why or Why not?
4. How does sharing your feelings help you to understand them better?

Directions:

Part II: One of the more prevalent feelings that linger in grief and loss situations is sadness. When children hold this feeling of sadness inside of them without expressing how they are feeling, they may begin to isolate themselves and/or withdraw from others. Often times, it is difficult for children to express themselves without the guidance of the counselor or another trusted person.

Hand out the copies of the activity page, *Expressing My Feelings of Sadness*, to the students. Say to them: *Sometimes, when people have very strong feelings, especially like sad, lonely, or scared feelings, they hold these feelings inside and do not talk about them. Think about a bottle of carbonated soda. You shake it up and all the bubbles foam around inside, but once you open up the bottle, it explodes! It's the same way with feelings. The longer you hold your feelings inside, the more they explode like a bottle of soda when you let them out. It is best to be able to express your feelings, or let them out, so that you can deal with them.*

Earlier, we talked about many different kinds of feelings that you might experience. Sadness is one of the feelings that children often hold inside, and do not talk about with others. This can cause feelings of loneliness and withdrawal (or separating yourself) from others.

In front of you is an activity page called, "Expressing My Feelings of Sadness." Sometimes, it is easier to write about your strong feelings before trying to talk about them. I would like for each of you to answer the questions on this activity page. Write down whatever comes to your mind. You will have an opportunity to talk about your feelings later if you choose to. Give the students 10-15 minutes to write their answers, depending on the age level of the group.

Discussion Questions: Part II

1. How did it feel to be able to write down your feelings?
2. What are some of the things you do when you feel sad?
3. Who are some of the people with whom you can express your sadness and/or other feelings that you might have?
4. Why is it important to not hide your sadness?
5. How did this activity help you to become more aware of your feelings?

Alternative Activities:

Materials:

paper, crayons and/or colored markers

Directions:

Write the feeling words that are listed in Part I on the board or flipchart. Instruct the students as follows:

- Draw a picture that describes your sadness and/or any of the other feeling words listed above. Who is in your picture? What are you doing? What colors are you using? Write about your picture (optional).
- Write a poem about your feelings of sadness, confusion, loneliness, or any of the other feelings listed above.

Note to Counselors: Students may share their pictures and/or poems with the other group members, if they feel comfortable. If any student does not want to discuss his or her picture and/or poem, you may choose to discuss their work and feelings in an individual session.

Discussion Questions:
(to use with Alternative Activities)

1. How did it feel to draw and/or write about your sadness (or other feeling that you drew and/or wrote about)?
2. Explain this statement: Sadness is not a "bad" feeling; it just doesn't feel good.
3. Did it help you to express your feelings? Explain.
4. How did it help you to share your feelings with others in the group? Did it help you to also share their feelings?
5. What did you learn from this activity?

EXPRESSING MY FEELINGS

Complete the following sentences:

1. I feel sad when
   _____

2. One time I felt sad was
   _____

3. When I feel sad, I
   _____

4. Someone I can share my sadness with is _____
   because _____

5. It doesn't feel good to hide my sadness inside of me because
   _____

6. Feeling sad is an "okay" feeling because
   _____

7. One of the feelings I have, besides feeling sad, is
   _____

8. Another feeling I sometimes have is
   _____

9. Someone I can share these other feelings with is _____
   because _____

COPING SKILLS
Dealing With Grief and Loss

Purpose:
to understand the stages of grief in dealing with loss

Objective:
Through learning about the stages of grief, students will gain an understanding of what they are going through in the grief and loss process.

Materials:
whiteboard or flipchart

Directions/Activity:

Children are especially vulnerable in dealing with loss. When parents "don't want to talk about the loss" or feel that the child is "okay" because he or she is not talking about it, the child may be holding in the feelings of grief for a longer period of time. The need to express these feelings is important in order to help the child move through the stages of grief. Whether it is the death of a person or a pet, the child experiences feelings of anxiety and sadness and needs to have a supportive environment in which to deal with these issues.

Reactions to loss may include: difficulty sleeping, loss of concentration in school, reverting to earlier phases of childhood (thumb sucking, bed wetting, temper tantrums, etc.); and/or displaying sadness, anger, or guilt. Children may need to deal with underlying fears of anything having to do with death. They may often feel "sick" or become overly "clingy." Sometimes, children will display silliness, or joke around, if the issues are too difficult to handle. In small group counseling, counselors must be sensitive to the needs of the children, and be aware that group members may display varying reactions.

The following *Stages of Grief* activity is to be used to work with small groups of children (approximately 5-6 students) who are working through issues of grief and loss. This lesson may cover two sessions, depending upon the needs of the group and how the discussion flows. It is suggested that a permission form describing the group session(s) be sent home to the parent/guardian. It should be signed and returned to the counselor. Before you begin, emphasize with the students: *What you say in here, stays in here.* It is important to keep confidentiality within the group.

Talk about the stages of grief with the students, one stage at a time. Write the words on the board or flipchart before defining them. As you go over each stage, be aware of the reactions of the various students.

1. *Denial:* Acting as though it didn't happen; or, smiling, laughing, or acting silly rather than showing sadness
2. *Anger:* Being mean, irritable, grumpy, annoyed, or moody
3. *Bargaining:* Deciding that if I act nicer or better, the person who is lost will return
4. *Depression:* Feeling sad, withdrawn, lonely, helpless, or hopeless
5. *Acceptance:* Thinking that I can get through this and smile, that life will go on and I will be okay, or that I will accept it even if I don't like it

Tell the students the following: *Stages move around. You may be in one stage and then move to another. You may move on to the next stage, or possibly, even go back to the same stage as before. You may reach different stages at different times. Although there isn't a definite order, you must move through the stages. Otherwise, you can get stuck at one stage. For example, if you don't move through the anger stage, you will remain angry; if you don't work through your sadness or depression, you will remain sad and depressed. It is important to know that these stages are a part of healing. As you become aware of them and move through them, you <u>will</u> heal.*

Tell the students: *We will be talking further about the stages of grief. Through our discussion, you will gain an awareness of your feelings. Remember, that what we say in here stays in here. This is a safe place to talk about your feelings.*

After you feel that the students understand the concepts of the five stages of grief, discuss the following questions with them. Some children will want to talk. Others may not, and that is okay. You may be able to draw them into the discussion later in the session. They will also gain a lot from listening. Do not allow one child to monopolize the conversation to the exclusion of other group members.

After each question has been discussed, ask the students if they know what stage they are talking about. (Although there are a number of questions under each stage, you may choose to ask each question separately.)

QUESTIONS

Is there, or was there, a time when you felt that your loss really didn't happen? Did you try to pretend it all wasn't real? Did you laugh and play and act as if everything was okay? Tell us about these times. Why do you think this is, or was, happening?

This stage is about **Denial**.

Do you ever feel sad or lonely? Do you stay to yourself a lot of the time? Do you think that others don't, or won't, understand? Do you feel like nothing is going to help you feel better? Tell us about these times. Why do you think this is, or was, happening?

This stage is about **Depression**.

Do you sometimes feel irritable or grumpy? Do you act mean towards others or say mean things? Do you ever feel like you are in a bad mood, but maybe don't know why? Why do you think this is, or was, happening?

This stage is about **Anger**.

Do you try to act especially nice or try to be perfect so that maybe the person who is lost will return? Do you sometimes think that if you do your very best in school, keep your room neat, or maybe act really kind to your brother or sister that everything will be the way it used to be? Why do you think this is, or was, happening?

This stage is about **Bargaining**.

Do you now feel that even though you don't like what happened, you will be able to accept it? Do you feel that you will be okay and that life will go on? Can you look ahead to positive things and happenings in your life? How do you think you reached this stage, or are working on it now? (Emphasize that in this stage you still love the person who is gone, but you cannot change what has occurred.)

This stage is about **Acceptance**.

Extension Activity:

Say to the students: *Draw a picture of where you are now, i.e., what stage you think you are in, or how you feel.*

Discussion Questions:

1. What did you learn about the stages of grief that you didn't already know?
2. What did you learn about yourself? Did it help you to understand how you are thinking, feeling, and/or acting?
3. What did you learn about others in your group?
4. Did this discussion help you realize that you are not alone in your feelings of grief and loss?
5. Did it help you to share your feelings with other group members?
6. Is there a parent, grandparent, aunt or uncle, brother or sister, or trusted neighbor with whom you can share your feelings?
7. Is there a trusted teacher, counselor, or other person in your school with whom you can share your feelings?

A CHANCE TO SAY "GOOD-BYE"
Dealing With Grief and Loss

Purpose:

to give children a chance to express themselves and say, "good-bye" to their loved ones through letter writing

Objective:

Students will be able to express their thoughts and feelings in a letter to their loved ones, thus having the opportunity to say "good-bye" in their own words.

Materials:

a copy of the activity page, *My Special Letter of Love*, for each student

Directions:

It is difficult for children or adolescents to believe that a special person in their lives is gone. Perhaps the loss of a loved one was sudden and there was no time to say "good-bye." As they go through the time of sadness, or grieving, they may be holding on to thoughts that they need to be able to express. Children need to have the opportunity to write a personal letter to the person who died. They may choose to share it with the other group members by reading it out loud, or by just telling them what's its about. Or, they may not. They may choose to take it home to share with members of their family. Or, they may not. They may choose to take it home and keep it just for themselves. Or, they may not. They just might choose to write it, remember the feelings in their hearts, and then throw it away. The choice is theirs.

No matter what the students choose to do with their letters, the writing process itself is the important part. Being able to share their feelings, and "talk" to the person through letter writing, is the part that takes them a step further through the grieving process.

The following letter-writing activity, *My Special Letter of Love*, may be experienced in a small group setting of 4-8 students (depending on the age of the child or adolescent), or in may be done in individual counseling.

Note to Counselors: This session may take about 45 minutes in order to give the students the necessary time to write their letters and then process the activity. As valuable as the letter writing is in itself, going over the Discussion Questions with the students is an important part of the counseling process. The idea of sharing their thoughts and feelings with one or more family members is brought out a few times throughout the discussion period. Although it is an important step to be able for the students to share with their family, it is emphasized, not assigned.

Begin the session by saying: *You are meeting together as a group, because you are all going through the loss of a loved one. Although every situation is a personal one, and some of your experiences may be different, many parts of the grieving process, or times of sadness, are the same. When a person you love dies, you may feel like there is something you would like to say, or have wanted to say if you'd had the chance.*

Today you will be given the time to write a special letter to the person you have lost. In it you may write your private thoughts and feelings – anything you want to say. It is your own personal letter. When you are finished writing, you may do whatever you choose with the letter. You may share it with the group, if that's what you want to do, but you don't have to. You may take it home with you and share it with your family, if that's what you'd like to do. You can take it home and keep it only for yourself in a special, private place; and you can also take it out and read it from time to time, if that's what you want to do; but you don't have to. You can even tear it up and throw it away, keeping the memory in your heart, if you want to. The choice is yours. You can do anything with your letter that you choose. The important thing is to be able to express your thoughts and feelings, rather than keeping them stuffed down deep inside.

Note to Counselors: If any student chooses not to share with the rest of the group, or chooses to tear up his or her letter, take the time after the group session is over to speak with that child before he or she leaves school. Discuss with the child how he or she is feeling, and emphasize the value of sharing these feelings with his or her family members.

Note to Counselors: It is a good idea to invite all of the group members to a follow-up short session the next day to see if any of the students are in need of individual counseling.

Hand out a copy of the activity page, *My Special Letter of Love*, to each student. Help them find a private space just for themselves in which to do their letter writing. The students will probably need about 15-20 minutes to write their letters depending on their ages. When they are finished, give the students an opportunity to share with the other group members by either reading their letters or saying something about them. Remind the students that what they do with their letters is up to them.

Discussion Questions:

1. Grieving is a period of sadness that follows losing someone you love. How does writing a letter to your loved one help you through the grieving process, or time of sadness?
2. How did you feel when you were writing your letter?
3. Did you feel any different when you finished writing your letter than you did before you began?
4. Why might it be a good choice to share your letter with one or more members of your family? How does sharing your thoughts and feelings help you?
5. If your choice is to keep the letter in a special, private place, just for yourself, could you choose at another time to take it out and share it with a family member?
6. If your choice is to tear up the letter and throw it away, could you still share your thoughts and feelings with members of your family at another time, if you want to?
7. What do you think you have learned from this lesson that might help you through your sadness?
8. How are you feeling right now as the group session draws to a close? *Take the time to have each group member answer this question before ending the counseling session.*

Note to Counselors: If any of the students appear to need some special alone time, make arrangements to see them in individual counseling.

MY SPECIAL LETTER OF LOVE

PARENT PERMISSION LETTER
Grief and Loss

Because of the sensitivity of issues of grief and loss, it is advisable to send a parent permission letter home to be signed by the parent/guardian. The following sample letter may be used or modified to meet your needs.

Dear Parents,

The counseling program at our school offers individual counseling, classroom guidance, parent-teacher conferences, and small group sessions that deal with specific concerns. Topics such as making friends, peer relationships, communication skills, decision-making skills, conflict resolution, and handling peer pressure are offered.

Your child has been invited to join one of the groups that deals with communicating in the family. Many students feel that the concerns they are having are unique. In the group, they discover that there are others who have the same problems they do. For students who have been through a grief and loss situation, it is often a comfort to learn how to adjust to the situation and communicate better with family members.

Your son/daughter, _____ has expressed an interest in being a part of this group. Please sign and return this letter with your child. If you have any questions or concerns, please call me at (phone number).

Sincerely,

(Name)
Counselor

_____ _____
Parent Signature   Date

ABOUT THE AUTHOR

Roxanne Zusmer, a native of Miami, Florida, holds a Masters degree in Mental Health Counseling and an Education Specialist degree in Educational Leadership. Previously a classroom teacher, Roxanne worked as a school counselor form 1985 to 2009, instilling innovative programs, character education, and life training skills, as well as parent education and community involvement. She served as adjunct professor at St. Thomas University in Miami and presented workshops and seminars both locally and nationally.

Roxanne has made a significant contribution to the counseling profession having served as president of the Florida School Counselor Association and the Florida Association for Specialists in Group Work, as well as Elementary Vice-President of the American School Counselor Association. She has been honored as Elementary Counselor of the Year at the local, state, and national levels. Roxanne is the author of the award winning book, *Mr. Germain Goes To Antarctica*, which promotes character education and environmental awareness, and a children's book, *Looking for the End of the Rainbow*.

Roxanne is a certified "Train-the-Trainer" with Active Parenting, Inc. She is available for workshops for parents, counselors, and teachers in areas of parenting (toddlers through teens); cooperative divorce; active teaching; academic success; and creative counseling techniques.

If your heart is in Social-Emotional Learning, visit us online.

Come see us at
www.InnerchoicePublishing.com

Our web site gives you a look at all our other Social-Emotional Learning-based books, free activities, articles, research, and learning and teaching strategies. Every week you'll get a new Sharing Circle topic and lesson.

INNERCHOICE Publishing

15079 Oak Chase Court
Wellington, FL 33414

www.ingramcontent.com/pod-product-compliance
Lightning Source LLC
Chambersburg PA
CBHW081939170426
43202CB00018B/2952